WINDOW TO THE FUTURE

WINDOW TO THE FUTURE

The Golden Age of Television Marketing and Advertising

By Steve Kosareff

CHRONICLE BOOKS

SAN FRANCISCO

Library of Congress Cataloging-in-Publication Data available.

ISBN 0-8118-4632-6

Manufactured in Hong Kong
Design by John Barretto

Distributed in Canada by Raincoast Books
9050 Shaughnessy Street
Vancouver, BC V6P 6E5

10 9 8 7 6 5 4 3 2 1

Chronicle Books LLC
85 Second Street
San Francisco, California 94105

www.chroniclebooks.com

GRACIE: "Now in *this* commercial, I want Harry Von Zell to pose with me to show how *much* you can *see* on Motorola's big, beautiful Extended Area screen! I'll admit George is much prettier than Harry . . . but on the other hand, Harry has much more of that BIG LOOK we want here!"

GEORGE: "Gracie is very proud of our BIG LOOK Motorola TV. She also likes our neighbors. So this is what she worked out. She put our Motorola in our picture window. Now our neighbors can enjoy our bigger, brighter BIG LOOK television at the same time *we* do!"

CONTENTS

	Introduction	**6**
Ch. 1	Television Fantastique – Even Without a Set to Watch	9
Ch. 2	Television Opportune – A World Wide Open	**21**
Ch. 3	All I Want for Christmas Is . . .	69
Ch. 4	Television Blazon – Color in a Black-and-White World	85
Ch. 5	Television Ballyhoo – The Medium on a Fishhook	**135**
Ch. 6	Television Intoxicant	153
Ch. 7	Television Celebrity – On the Big Screen but in *Front* of the Little Screen	**163**
Ch. 8	Television Imprint – Mother's Little Helper	171
	Acknowledgments	**176**

INTRODUCTION

It sits at attention, at your beck and call, in at least one room in your home. In fact, according to statistics, you are likely to own more than one, and in many homes, one is always within sight. It provides news and entertainment whenever you want it, and yet even the lowly refrigerator commands more respect. For over a generation we have taken television for granted. Around the turn of the twentieth century, television was still just a fantasy. But many had a persistent dream that it would someday become a reality, and the concept of television was revered. Then again, TV critics hadn't been invented yet. But even after they were, proliferating along with the number of sets manufactured and programs available, the magic of simply *receiving* thirty pictures a second (which persistence of vision seamlessly perceives as continuous motion) continued to amaze and delight those who were alive during the Golden Age of television sets, from the late 1940s through the early 1960s, when they were first installed in homes in great numbers.

Marketing and promotional materials during this era created their own form of fantasy for the medium as it made ever deeper inroads into American culture. Lavishly illustrated advertisements for *a hundred* American television set manufacturers in the 1950s (compared to the handful today, few of which are U.S. owned) spoke to the emotional, if not the performing, power of their sets in large-subscription weekly magazines like *Life, Look, The*

Saturday Evening Post, and *Colliers*. Ironically, the success of television, and of the ads the magazines ran, led to the demise of the weeklies. Subscriptions dropped as advertisers and the public stopped reading and started watching. The consequences were so dramatic that *Colliers,* one of the largest-subscription weekly magazines in the first half of the twentieth century, printed its last issue in January 1957; others limped along through the 1960s until most also met the same fate or, if they survived, published pale versions of their former selves. From then on, people received most of their world news and entertainment electronically. Television became part of our everyday routine, and the magic of the medium faded for many.

But not for all. Some became custodians, maintaining their love of the magic box and its ability to receive "pictures" out of thin air for decades, even though few others understood or remembered the phenomenon of television's Golden Age. Ironically, the introduction of another medium, the Internet, would network these "televisionaires."

In 1998 I logged on to the Internet for the first time. Through it I made contact with fellow television aficionados and set collectors. As a result of meeting these individuals, I researched and drafted a proposal for a national television museum that I hope to bring into being. The museum will celebrate the early history of the television medium, its fantasy in literature, its first experimental equipment, memorable sets produced for sale to the public from 1939 to 1970, its marketing and sales materials and ephemera, and, of course, its programming. Until ground is broken for that venue, I have written this book as the first in what I hope is a long series on the history of the television medium.

This book covers a century of television in fact and fantasy—beginning with the television device's first appearance in print around 1870 to the last classic U.S.–manufactured sets through 1970—telling its story through marketing and print advertising materials. Although advertisements for television sets appeared concurrently with the medium's public introduction at the 1939 New York World's Fair, and although World War II's intervention produced futuristic ads that promised sets once the war ended, the bulk of advertisements started shortly after the end of the war in 1946. Initially few and far between, television set ads picked up steam in 1948 and appeared regularly thereafter in all the large-subscription weeklies, where the widest possible audience would see them. I have looked at every *Collier's, Saturday Evening Post,* and *Life* magazine published during the boom years of television set sales, roughly 1946 to 1970. The marketing materials and ads in this book are from my collection and have been selected for their historical significance, production values, and/or their clever and unique ways of selling television sets.

"Television Fantastique" roughly covers the period from 1870 to 1946, when television sets progressed from a fantasy to a prototype to a commercial product that was available only on a limited basis to the wealthy who could afford them. Then World War II not only halted production but restricted sales of high-ticket consumer items. "Television Opportune" overviews the period of the American television boom years that followed the war, roughly 1946 to 1970. "All I Want for Christmas Is . . . " celebrates television set ads in the 1950s with a holiday theme; "Television Blazon" introduces color television in the 1950s; "Television Ballyhoo" features ads that, although not created to sell television sets, included them or used some variation on a television theme to attract

readers' attention; "Television Intoxicant" recalls the beginning of the medium's long relationship with liquor; "Television Celebrity" remembers movie stars pitching a medium they could not yet work in; and, finally, "Television Imprint" presents a view of the medium and the set's relationship to American families in the 1950s.

By 1960, with the large-subscription weeklies losing their audiences and/or beginning to fold and black-and-white television sales reaching saturation, the quality of ads produced during the 1950s television boom years had disappeared. With rare exceptions they continued into the 1960s, but even the color television groundswell of that decade did not inspire ads as lavishly produced and as cleverly conceived as those from the 1950s. By 1970, inexpensively produced Japanese television sets had made enough of an inroad in the United States that many American companies had already thrown in the towel and stopped manufacturing television sets or were themselves sold abroad. It was the end of an era for American television sets and their ads, but one that I have attempted to recapture in these pages.

Even if you do not have television fever as I and many others do, I hope you will find pleasure in the following pages as we celebrate the medium that was once known as the "window to the future."

Steve Kosareff
Santa Monica, California

1

TELEVISION FANTASTIQUE –
Even Without a Set to Watch

TELEVISION FANTASTIQUE
Even Without a Set to Watch

In 1870 the second part of Jules Verne's *20,000 Leagues Under the Sea* was published in soft cover in France. By the time the two-part hardcover book reached American shores in 1872, Lewis Mercier, its English translator, had deleted a quarter of the text, including what is likely the first printed description of a "distant vision" device. The 2001 translation of Verne's story by Frederick P. Walter restores this omission. Verne's imagination influenced many people, including his contemporary French futurist Albert Robida (pictured above), who parodied Verne's theme of Armageddon-like wars in his first illustrated science fiction book, *Les voyages très-extraordinaires de Saturnin Farandoul* (1879). However, two of Robida's trilogy of books regarding life in the twentieth century, *Le Vingtième Siecle* (The Twentieth Century) (1883) and *Le Vingtième Siecle—La Vie Electrique* (The Twentieth Century—The Electric Life) (1891), contain his illustrations of "distant vision" devices. Robida accurately predicted what people would see and do with television. His viewers watch scenes of war and sexuality and interactively shop and educate themselves. Interaction via television would thrive in artists' imaginations and illustrations from approximately the 1890s through the mid-1920s, with rough concepts of videophones and people literally reaching out to touch one another. In one stretch of the imagination, people are even able to transfer a strand of pearls over the ether. As fanciful as this was, the pinnacle of what people imagined for interactive television must be on the cover of the sheet music for *I Wish There Were a Television to Heaven (So I Could See My Mother Tonight)*. In it, a child tunes in a deceased relative from the hereafter. Illustrators such as Howard Brown and Henry Moore Picken fed people's fantasies about television with their beautiful covers for science and science fantasy magazines, many of them owned and edited by electronic media baron Hugo Gernsback, who was also another visionary and champion of early television.

Gernsback was born in Luxembourg to a wealthy family in 1885 (during the period that Albert Robida was illustrating his "distant vision" device). His father was a wholesaler of wines in Europe. An early boyhood fascination with things electrical led him to wire his parents' home for electricity (as British "father of television" John Logie Baird did) and later to study mathematics and electrical engineering at the Technikum in Bingen, Germany. Gernsback's other main interest was American culture, including Mark Twain, John Phillip Sousa, and "Wild West" comic books. He emigrated to the United States in 1904 and started his own battery company, which designed the first home radio set and successfully sold these until the United States entered World War I (at which time amateur radio transmissions were banned). Left holding $100,000 of apparently worthless electronic parts and equipment, his future looked bleak. But a stroke of marketing genius would change that. Gernsback came up with an idea to package the electronic parts into kits, with handbooks that told young boys how to build things like wireless telephones. The kits sold remarkably well and saved his business. Eventually the handbooks evolved into monthly science magazines with titles like *Modern Electrics* (with the first printed use of the word "television" in 1909), *Radio News, Science and Invention, Radio Listeners' Guide and Call Book, Television News,* and *Short Wave and Television*. They inspired not only boys (such as young Philo Farnsworth, who would later become one of the most prominent "fathers" of television), but also scientists, who believed that their electronic fantasies could be realized. Among Gernsback's professional admirers were radio's developer, Guglielmo Marconi; inventor Thomas Edison; electrical engineer and inventor Nikola Tesla; rocketry developer Robert Goddard; radio tube developer Lee DeForest; and RCA chief David Sarnoff. Paul O'Neil, writing in a July 26, 1963, *Life* magazine article on Gernsback, said that he had an "unabashed sense of theater" and ". . . not only prepare[d] the public mind for the 'wonders' of science but . . . [told] science . . . just what wonders it was about to produce."

Gernsback's *Radio News* magazine touted on its cover his New York radio station WRNY. WRNY conducted experimental television broadcasts in 1928 during the height of television's mechanical spinning-and-scanning disc craze (this system would eventually disappear altogether by the mid-1930s in favor of the more reliable operation and higher-resolution picture of all-electronic television), and *Radio News* published

articles and schematics designed to teach its readers how to build their own home receivers. Gernsback appeared on the November 1928 *Radio News* cover in a color illustration (rendered from a black-and-white photograph) that showed him watching his own experimental mechanical set in the comfort of his living room. Thirty-five years later, he would also be photographed for the 1963 *Life* article sporting a pair of his "teleyeglasses," which look like a prototype of a Game Boy visor (see page 66).

By the mid-1930s, sets were not yet commercially available (due to a need for some further "fine-tuning" development and to electronics manufacturers' desire to milk as much money as possible from radio receivers before television was unleashed on the public), but the motion picture industry had caught the television bug and began marketing to appeal to the public's fascination with the fantasy—and lack of knowledge—of television. It attempted to draw crowds to theaters with movie titles like *Trapped by Television, Television Spy,* and *Murder by Television.* It must have appeared to many that television could do just about anything. The television element in many of the films from this period usually took the form of two-way communication vis-à-vis a glorified videophone, such as that used in the 1935 British film *Transatlantic Tunnel.* Those whose knowledge of television

came from one of these movies might have assumed that since television could either hold you hostage, spy on you, or kill you, it must be a bad thing. These perceptions may well have played a subliminal part in the public's slow acceptance of the medium prior to World War II.

The initially poor sales of television sets was the result of more than just perception, however. Also playing a part were the high cost of sets; the small size of their pictures (compared to motion pictures); the poor viewing choices consisting of old newsreels and cheaply produced live programming (compared to the high-budget, high-quality network radio programs); and the very real possibility of electronic obsolescence (since broadcasting and reception standards had not been agreed upon by the various radio manufacturers). When the first sets went on sale in New York City concurrent with the opening of the 1939 World's Fair, people flocked to the five television exhibits where manufacturers had sets on display. Two of the bigger exhibits were created by RCA and General Electric, where people could not only see working television sets but also be televised to see themselves and others on-screen. Unfortunately, the novelty didn't translate into sales. The crowds at the fair's exhibits dwarfed those lining up outside dealers to get a peek, and those numbers were massive compared to those who entered the

stores and plunked down cold hard cash to buy sets. Sales weren't just poor, they were a disaster when New York's huge metropolitan population was taken into consideration: only eight hundred sets were sold by July of that year. Five thousand sat in warehouses. Sets were discounted, given to opinion makers (such as President Franklin Roosevelt—whose RCA set still sits in his Hyde Park home along the Hudson River in New York State), and even sold to RCA employees at discount, but to little avail. With the United States' involvement in World War II rapidly approaching and the government decree that essential manufacturers switch over to war-related goods, weapons, and machinery, television set production came to a halt, and all sets in the process of being manufactured, whether completed or not, were shelved in warehouses for the duration of the war—as much as six long years for some.

Even without television sets being produced and sold, in order to maintain their FCC television licenses during the war, broadcasters continued to send a certain amount of programming out into the ether in New York, Los Angeles, and a few other large cities. And there was an audience to receive the programs, albeit a small one, with an estimated five thousand sets in use across the country. After the United States entered the war, in January 1942, televi-

sion even did its part in the war effort by broadcasting civil defense and air raid training programs in New York and Los Angeles and eventually entertaining wounded veterans recouping in military hospitals. Many people who had not seen the World's Fair television exhibits were now getting their first look at the medium. Anticipating a successful end to the war, manufacturers geared up to sell postwar television sets by whetting the public's appetite with futuristic ads depicting them in homes, often with giant-screen images on walls, or in industrial settings, where the all-seeing eye of a camera and monitor could allow an industrial plant manager to keep tabs on an operation.

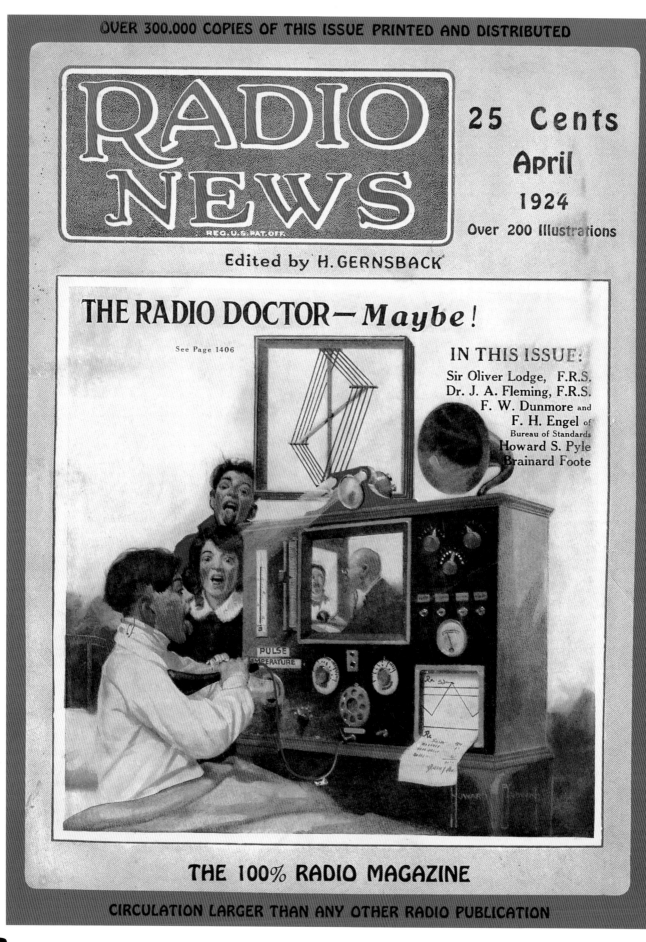

THE 100% RADIO MAGAZINE

CIRCULATION LARGER THAN THAT OF ANY OTHER RADIO PUBLICATION

RADIO PHONE
WRNY
STATION

RADIO NEWS

REG. U.S. PAT. OFF.

Edited by HUGO GERNSBACK

25 Cents

MAY

Over 200 Illustrations

SOON—

*"THIS IS
SO SUDDEN"*

RADIO'S GREATEST MAGAZINE

EXPERIMENTER PUBLISHING COMPANY, NEW YORK, PUBLISHERS OF
SCIENCE and INVENTION   RADIO REVIEW   AMAZING STORIES   RADIO INTERNACIONAL

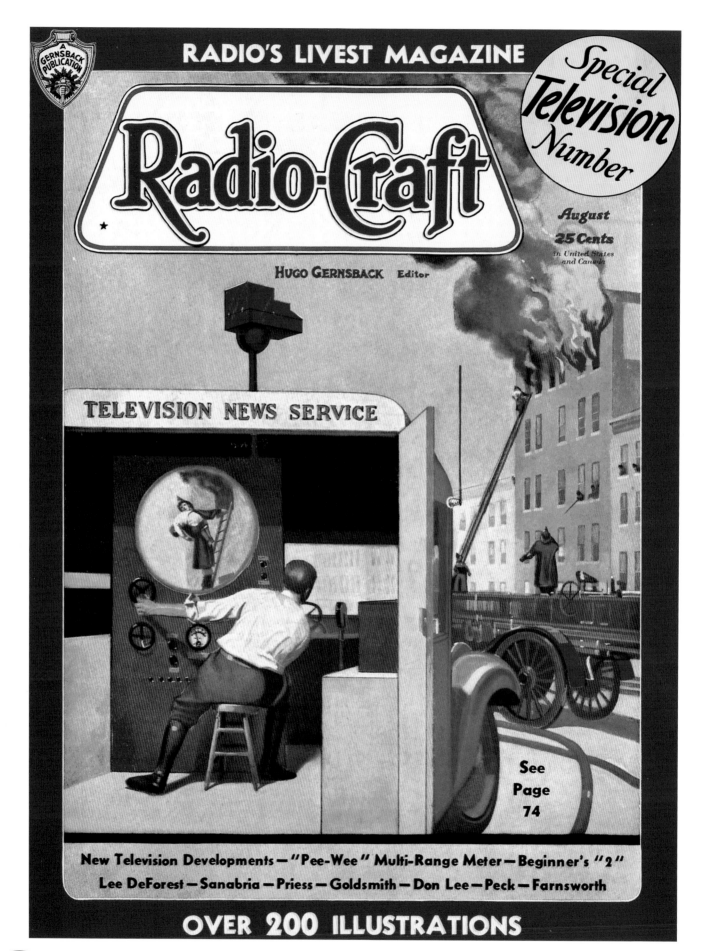

RADIO'S LIVEST MAGAZINE

Special Television Number

Radio-Craft

HUGO GERNSBACK Editor

August
25 Cents
in United States
and Canada

TELEVISION NEWS SERVICE

See
Page
74

New Television Developments — "Pee-Wee" Multi-Range Meter — Beginner's "2"
Lee DeForest — Sanabria — Priess — Goldsmith — Don Lee — Peck — Farnsworth

OVER 200 ILLUSTRATIONS

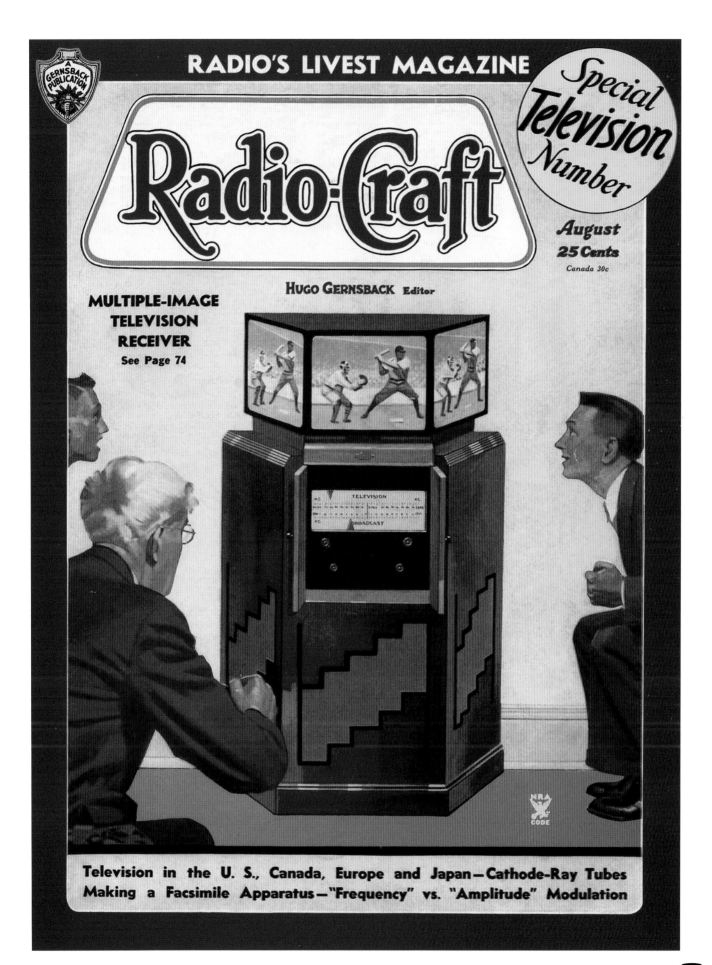

RADIO'S LIVEST MAGAZINE

Special Television Number

Radio-Craft

August
25 Cents
Canada 30c

HUGO GERNSBACK Editor

MULTIPLE-IMAGE
TELEVISION
RECEIVER
See Page 74

Television in the U. S., Canada, Europe and Japan—Cathode-Ray Tubes
Making a Facsimile Apparatus—"Frequency" vs. "Amplitude" Modulation

2

TELEVISION OPPORTUNE –
A World Wide Open

TELEVISION OPPORTUNE –
A World Wide Open

Shortly after the end of World War II, in June 1946, the first television sets for sale since the war began became available. With some dusting off and tweaking of components, the first sets were those that had been warehoused for the war's duration. And the public—which had been denied major consumer items during the war—was hungry for the big, expensive ticket items they had, at least in part, fought the war for. For television manufacturers, the war did bring about an unexpected benefit: concentrated laboratory research further developed electronics and tubes for radar and oscilloscopes that could now be put to use in television sets. As the manufacturers reconverted their production plants for civilian use, they incorporated these new electronic developments into the first postwar sets to be built. Sales continued to be slow, but as new and improved sets with bigger screen sizes arrived at dealers over the next several years and once NBC began producing the expensive and lavish Milton Berle variety show in 1948, people began to take notice of the medium. Initially, neighbors and friends gathered at the home of a person who owned a set or at local bars where innkeepers could quantify the expensive sets by the increased number of drinks they sold after sets were purchased, but as this became an inconvenience, people increasingly purchased sets of their own.

Television sets were marketed two ways: as budget table receivers for under $200 or as sets combined with radios and phonographs in large, beautiful, expensive wood cabinets for $500. Ads targeting the wealthy who could afford the $500 sets featured people formally dressed in tuxedos and evening gowns, which sent the unmistakable message that they were better than the average, middle-class Joe who watched his $200 set (if he could afford one) in his undershirt and work pants. Ads for expensive television entertainment centers would continue to use formally dressed models almost exclusively even into the 1960s during the color television boom. But, did *anyone* really watch television in formal wear?

In fact, most people weren't wealthy, and many couldn't afford even a budget set several years after the war was over, but RCA was there for them. It offered a television savings plan that, according to a September 1950 ad, would allow people to set aside money to buy a set at some future date. The giant picture tube in the ad bore less resemblance to a piggy bank than it did to a giant funnel, channeling consumers' money into RCA's pocket.

Set manufacturer Admiral attempted to bridge the gap, for those who could afford only a budget table model but wanted the luxury of a console, by introducing a "consolette" set with a cabinet constructed completely out of a plastic called Bakelite. Bakelite had previously been used to create small items like jewelry, but Admiral's set was the largest individual piece ever created. Durable and inexpensive to manufacture, the Bakelite sets mirrored the wood cabinets of their more expensive brothers. Many of the Bakelite cabinets survive today because they were resistant to just about every kind of wear and tear except cracking. Even then a set would have to be dropped from a substantial height or be hit with an object the weight of a piano in order to crack.

In 1950, just as black-and-white television set sales began to reach a critical mass, CBS publicly threw a wrench in the works by demonstrating its color television system in New York City on December 13. Like the late 1920s and early 1930s experimental black-and-white television systems, the CBS color system used a spinning disc with holes in it to scan an image, but in this case one with colored gels for each of the three primary colors. Unfortunately, also like the early black-and-white television systems, it was doomed from the start because it was partially mechanical, even though the color television picture it produced was quite good.

The next day, black-and-white television set manufacturers (who were just starting to reap the fruits of their long-term investments and were not about to hand over the growing television sales boom) banded together to fight the CBS color "conspiracy" by running an ad in the *New York Times* featuring a photograph of a boy and girl who appeared to be orphaned. In fact, according to the text of the ad, they were shunned by their peers and ashamed of their family because their parents didn't own a (black-and-white) television set. Eleanor Roosevelt—who had signed up as a representative of the ad's sponsor, the American Television Services and Manufacturers—was so incensed at the ad's degradation of families simply because they didn't own television sets that she wanted to publicly withdraw her involvement with the organization, even though the manufacturers had made a feeble attempt to neutralize the tasteless ad with an ". . . oh, by the way" fleeting reference to television's ability to educate children.

The 1950s saw the first use of television for other than entertainment purposes. As early as August 1953, RCA promoted its first small portable commercial camera for live monitoring, which was initially marketed to parents to watch their babies. Had VCRs been available to parents at the time they could have been used as nanny-cams decades sooner. However, the most successful monitoring purpose for small cameras was live surveillance of banking and industry. Medical exams via television, which had been theorized as early as April 1924 (see the *Radio News* cover, page 14), would also become a reality late in the decade, but only on a limited basis.

The breakout year for television set sales was 1951. Although each year's sales since 1946 had managed to top the previous year, the completion of the networks' transcontinental cable and telephone relay link that September created a tremendous desire to purchase sets. In the past, television viewers often saw network shows rebroadcast from grainy kinescopes (films shot off television monitor screens) days or weeks after their live airings because there was no direct network link to their local affiliated station. Now, with the completion of the transcontinental link, programs could be seen simultaneously from coast to coast in the high, clear resolution of their live broadcasts. Sales skyrocketed, and 6 million sets were sold that year alone—an amazing number when one considers that there were only 3.6 million in 1949. Now there were over 15.5 million television sets in the United States.

Lavishly illustrated "glamour" ads—featuring beautiful, alluring, fashionably dressed women—also reached their pinnacle during television's breakout year in 1951, but beautiful women would continue to be used liberally in television set ads through the decade and into the next. These women would appear, mostly alone, either cuddling, snuggling, or wrapping their arms around a particular advertiser's set. The message was clear: television sets are sexy. And the subtext was just as obvious: if you're a woman, you'll feel, if not look, as attractive as these women do, and if you're a man, you will be sexy by association and able to attract the opposite sex—if you buy *this* particular manufacturer's set.

To reel in those already married, and often with children, many advertisers relied on the "spellbound" effect. These ads portrayed the hypnotic, mesmerizing result their sets had on people, particularly children and husbands. In the 1950s, television sets were portrayed as seducers, the "other woman" that men longed for and the magician that transfixed children (see Chapter 8, "Television Imprint"). At least a television set was a woman that wives and mothers could control by closing the cabinet doors or pulling the plug. This "spellbound" technique was so widely used in ads it may also have caused a backlash. During the Communist witch-hunts of the 1950s, many people were concerned that the government was spying on them. And what better way to do it than through the one-eyed seducer? Many people speculated that if they could see someone through their set, the converse might also be true and someone might be watching *them*. It hardly mattered that to accomplish this there had to be a television *camera* in the equation.

As transistors began to replace tubes in the late 1950s, therefore reducing the weight and service required, portability was introduced. You couldn't yet plug a set into the cigarette lighter of your car, but you could take one to a mountain cabin (hopefully, there was a signal), the beach (for those not wishing to swim, perhaps?), or on a picnic. RCA, which had received a broadcast on an airplane from its affiliated NBC station in New York in 1940 as a public relations stunt to demonstrate the long (and, for the typical set owner, unlikely) distance from which an RCA set could receive a signal, would revisit the demonstration in 1958 and pick up a signal on a Boeing 707, which could travel at 600 miles per hour. "Tomorrow is here!" General Electric proclaimed as it redesigned its heavy, boxy table sets to have a lighter Space Age portability with curved, multihued plastic cabinets. Philco would go a step farther with its futuristic design of its Predicta models and their exposed picture tubes. One Predicta model even allowed the picture tube to be moved separately and apart from the cabinet via an early version of today's modern cable. Although the Predictas' electronics were poorly designed and the sets did not sell well, the uniqueness of their design has made them the most recognizable and highly sought-after collector sets today.

By the early 1960s, black-and-white television set sales had reached the saturation point and began to drop as color sets were now purchased in significant numbers, relegating the old black-and-whites (if they still worked) to bedrooms and dens across the country. Lavishly illustrated television ads in magazines for black-and-whites were now a thing of the past. But not without one last hurrah.

Motorola was planning to introduce a new black-and-white portable. It hired the New Center Studio in Detroit to design the ad campaign. The agency asked its artists to submit ideas detailing fantasy places to watch television. Illustrator Charles Schridde turned in a rendering of a man and woman who comfortably watch Motorola's portable on steps leading to a conical fireplace. The whole scene was staged in a *tree*. The ad ran in *Life* and *The Saturday Evening Post*. Motorola received so much positive feedback that when Schridde left the agency the company asked him to continue with a series of similar illustrations, which ran in both magazines from 1961 to 1963. Schridde's illustrations were epic visions of 1960s modernity, with elements of nature flowing freely in and out of homes as though they were organic to their settings. If the exterior of a home was not visible, water, plants, and/or rocks were incorporated in the interior. His designs were similar in style to many homes built in an exclusive desert enclave during that period. Schridde's illustrations may have also been some grand residential wish fulfillment.

Decades later he moved to that enclave: Palm Springs, California.

ADMIRAL
Triple Thrill

FM·AM RADIO

2-SPEED PHONOGRAPH

MAGIC MIRROR TELEVISION

Complete

HOME ENTERTAINMENT

ALL IN *One*

LUXURIOUS CONSOLE

$549⁵⁰
WALNUT

*Plus Installation and Fed. tax.
Mahogany or blonde cabinet extra.
Prices slightly higher in south.*

From Admiral . . . comes this triple thrill in complete home entertainment. **MAGIC MIRROR TELEVISION** brings you steady, mirror-clear pictures on a big 10″ direct-view screen . . . the clearest pictures of them all! Super-powered by 29 tubes (including rectifiers) to assure dependable performance even in outlying areas. Complete channel coverage. Here, too, is a powerful **FM-AM RADIO** including the finest features in static-free FM as engineered by Admiral. New **2-SPEED AUTOMATIC PHONOGRAPH** plays standard as well as the sensational new L.P. (long play) "microgroove" records. Imagine! 45 minutes of music . . . equivalent to a standard 6-record album . . . all from a single 12″ record. Truly a triple-thrill . . . all combined in a breathtakingly beautiful cabinet only 48 inches wide! See it! Hear it! Today!

AMERICA'S SMART SET *Admiral*

Supreme Moment!

when Zenith **Black Magic** Television comes into your life

You've known great moments in your life. You've lived in an age of marvels. But there's an experience coming your way—an experience so dramatic—so unbelievably out of the world, as to make all others seem commonplace.

It's not just television you're seeing...it's the miracle of Black Magic Television, made possible through Zenith's amazing discovery of the Blaxide Tube.

It's the thrill of seeing pictures so clear, so photographically life-like that you hardly believe your eyes. Pictures free from eye-straining glare or blur even in daylight or fully lighted rooms, as medical authorities recommend viewing.

And now for '51—wonder of wonders—the new Zenith reflection-proof feature added to make viewing even more perfect. Now you see pictures utterly free from window and room-light reflections at normal viewing position—truly, television's newest miracle. Be sure—be very sure—that when you invest in television—you guard against after-regrets.

Be sure to examine these features combined only in Zenith: Your choice of Giant Circle or rectangular type picture. Built-in "Picturemagnet" aerial. One-knob automatic tuning. New Magic "Lazy Bones" remote control to switch channels from your easy chair. (Optional at slight extra cost on all new Zenith® Television Receivers.) Connection for Phonevision† and built-in provision for tuner strips to receive the proposed new ultra-high frequencies on present standards.

Be sure you buy with the knowledge that you possess the most advanced television known to modern science.

†If and when this great Zenith development is approved as a commercial service and thereby is made available on present standards, unit may be attached to bring high-class, costly television programs right into your home.

The Magic of Quality...

...NEVER MORE APPARENT THAN NOW
IN DRAMATIC NEW ZENITH TELEVISION

with the World's Finest <u>Full-Focus</u> Picture!

Renowned for sheer quality the world over— Zenith now achieves TV's most spectacular advance in *Picture Quality*. The long-time dream of Radionic Science is realized with *The World's Finest full-focus TV picture,* a picture that stays *entirely* in focus *all* the time! Only Zenith can bring you such realism in a television picture. And Zenith is first again with the amazing "Electronex" Tube—to make true realism an accomplished fact.

Blur, distortion and edge-fading are nuisances of the past. Zenith's remarkable new "Electronex" Tube with the built-in Radionic® lens compensates for variations in line voltage that impair performance in ordinary sets. Truly, here at last is completely automatic focusing to add greatly to your TV enjoyment.

Only Zenith Television Has All This!

Provision for presently authorized color with connection for auxiliary color receiver. • *Provision for UHF.* Provision for simple insertion of tuner strips (takes 15 minutes). • *Clearest Picture Known.* New "Electronex" Picture Tube automatically assures full-focus picture over entire viewing area. • *New Distance-Reception.* Fringe Lock produces and permanently holds finest pictures ever seen, even in weak or outlying signal areas. Set it once for best reception and forget it. • *Minimum Reflection.* Tilted face plate and wide angle frame assures a perfect picture from practically anywhere in the room. • *Simple Automatic Tuning.* One-knob automatic Turret Tuner brings in perfect quality pictures and sound at one simple twist. • *Connection for Auxiliary Color Set.*

New Zenith "Kipling"
TV-Radio-Phonograph Console

Model J2868R. 17-inch (146 sq. in.) "Electronex" Tube screen. Cobra-Matic® record-player. FM-AM radio. Beautiful Sheraton cabinet of Mahogany veneer.

Zenith Radio Corporation, Chicago 39, Illinois
Over 30 Years of "Know-How" in Radionics® Exclusively

Also makers of Zenith "Royal" and "Super Royal" Hearing Aids. Small, compact, beautifully designed. Money back guarantee. Sold only through authorized dealers at $75.

World's Most Advanced TV and Record Playing...

ZENITH QUALITY Black Magic TV

Plus Cobra-Matic Record Player with Pitch and Tempo Control

Once you witness the marvel that is the Zenitheatre TV-Radio-Phonograph, you know there is something new, something different, something better, in complete home entertainment.

In the Zenitheatre, you enjoy TV so far advanced that you have not the slightest concern about the wisdom of your investment. Zenith's remarkable developments in screen size and picture clarity bring out every detail with thrilling realism. You change programs from your easy chair, with Zenith's marvelous Lazy Bones Remote Control. You have built-in provision for tuner strips to receive the new Ultra-High Frequencies on present standards, and a connection provided for Phonevision.†

And because you love recorded music, you are simply thrilled with Zenith's

The Music Lover's Dream

Cobra-Matic. The first—the only—automatic record-player that lets you play all records at the exact speed they were recorded...enables you to adjust speed for perfect pitch, tempo and timbre—the "tone color" that gives great voices and masterfully played instruments their full, breath-taking beauty. You can play not only 33⅓, 45, 78, but thousands of intermediate speeds from 10 to 85, including the coming new 16 R.P.M. records!

Why merely dream of all the glorious home entertainment that can be yours? You want it—your family deserves it—right now. Today, discover how easily it can be yours in a Zenitheatre TV-Radio-Phonograph. Your Zenith dealer invites you.

Above, New Zenith® "Whitman" TV-Radio-Phonograph with 17 inch (146 sq. in.) rectangular tube screen; Cobra-Matic Record-Player; Long-distance® AM and Super-Sensitive FM radio. Period cabinet, genuine Mahogany veneers.

†If and when this great Zenith development is approved as a commercial service and thereby is made available on present standards, unit may be attached to bring high-class, costly programs right into your home.

THE DRESS . . . A **BLACK MAGIC** ORIGINAL
BY *Sophie* OF SAKS FIFTH AVENUE

Zenith Radio Corporation, Chicago 39, Illinois • Over 30 Years of "Know-How" in Radionics® Exclusively • Also Makers of Fine Hearing Aids   ©1951

29

Enchanted Evening by Zenith

The Setting: You...Your guests...**1951 Black Magic TV**
with Reflection-Proof Screen

Your guests arrive...You try not to look too obviously proud as you switch on your new Zenith...Conversation ripples to a whisper...

Then—a flood of excited comment..."I can scarcely believe what I'm seeing!"..."I had no idea television could be so big and real"..."It's so wonderfully clear and steady"...

Then comes the magic moment! Never leaving your easy chair, you change programs with Zenith's "Lazy Bones," the amazing remote control that fits in your palm. Click...click...click...you change one program after another, no knob to touch or re-tune!

"It's sheer Black Magic" someone exclaims. And it is...Your magic passport to enchanted evenings from now on, is this incredibly fine, incredibly beau-

tiful new Zenith for 1951. Your Zenith dealer invites you to a pre-view...now!

*   *   *

"Must see" before you buy any TV: Zenith's new 2-in-1 screen with Reflection-Proof Blaxide Tube. Bans room reflections as well as glare, even in fully lighted surroundings, as doctors recommend viewing. Gives you two picture shapes in one set (Giant Circle or rectangular type) at the touch of a switch! New "Super-Range" Chassis gets programs far clearer in outlying locations. Pre-tuned Picturemagnet built-in antenna needs no adjusting. All this plus built-in provision for tuner strips to receive proposed Ultra-High Frequencies on present standards. Glorious new cabinets of lifetime beauty and quality.

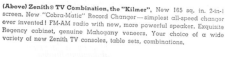

(Above) Zenith® TV Combination, the "Kilmer", New 165 sq. in. 2-in-1 screen. New "Cobra-Matic" Record Changer—simplest all-speed changer ever invented! FM-AM radio with new, more powerful speaker. Exquisite Regency cabinet, genuine Mahogany veneers. Your choice of a wide variety of new Zenith TV consoles, table sets, combinations.

New Zenith "Zephyr"® Table radio for Long-Distance AM reception. New Giant Dial-Speaker combines larger, extra-powerful Alnico-5 speaker with easy-tuning dial. "Flexo-Grip" handle. Walnut, Ebony or White plastic cabinet.

New Zenith "Universal"® Super-powered standard broadcast portable—with tone richness comparable to big consoles. Smart luggage-type case in buffalo-grained black or brown. Works on battery, AC, DC.

ZENITH
•LONG DISTANCE• RADIO and TELEVISION

Over 30 Years of "Know-How" in Radionics® Exclusively • Zenith Radio Corp., Chicago 39, Ill. • Also Makers of America's Finest Hearing Aids ©1950

There's *Black Magic* in the Blaxide Tube

ZENITH'S AMAZING TELEVISION DISCOVERY

It's afternoon—you don't draw the shades. It's evening—you don't dim the lights. You twist one knob and Presto! the spectacular Glare-Ban "Black" (Blaxide) Tube, originated and perfected by Zenith*, brings you television pictures with startling new life-like clarity and detail, free from eyestraining glare and blur!

Everywhere, experts and set owners alike are calling it "Black Magic"—this amazing new way to view television in broad daylight or fully lighted rooms, the way medical authorities recommend.

Of course, Zenith has its own built-in aerial, the exclusive "Picturemagnet"... *plus* a new super-sensitive video circuit that assures you clear, steady pictures where many other sets fail. And *only* Zenith gives you both built-in provision for receiving the proposed ultra-high frequencies on present standards and connection for Phonevision†. Zenith engineering foresight *anticipates* the significant developments in television. Buy Zenith with confidence, today!

†When Phonevision is available, unit may be attached to bring such entertainment as first-run movies, Broadway plays, operas, etc., right into your home.

Above, New Zenith "Madison" TV-Radio-Phonograph

105 sq. in. Giant Circle Screen. 3-Way automatic record playing of all sizes and speeds. New Super-Sensitive FM, famous Long-Distance AM radio. Beautifully grained Mahogany veneer cabinet. You may choose from a wide variety of Zenith Television receivers priced from $219.95‡ to $625.00‡, plus Federal excise tax.

©1950

New Zenith "Major"
FM table radio. Opens a new world of radio enjoyment, with new Super-Sensitive FM reception. Works even where many AM or ordinary FM sets are practically useless! Big set tone quality, smart Walnut plastic cabinet. AC-DC. A terrific value. $39⁹⁵‡

New Zenith "Zephyr"*
AM table radio. Super powerful long distance performer. Has exclusive Consoltone®, Wavemagnet®, Alnico 5 Speaker, Flexo-Grip handle. Sparkling Ebony or Swirl Walnut plastic cabinet, "soft gold" grille, large circular chrome dial. AC-DC. $34⁹⁵‡

ZENITH
•LONG DISTANCE• **RADIO and TELEVISION**

THE ROYALTY OF RADIO AND TELEVISION

‡Prices subject to change without notice. West Coast and far South prices slightly higher. *Reg. U. S. Pat. Off.
Over 30 Years of "Know-How" in Radionics® Exclusively • Zenith Radio Corp., Chicago 39, Ill. • Also Makers of America's Finest Hearing Aids

But One Standard...Quality

Magnificently Yours in the Dramatic New Zenith Television
WITH THE WORLD'S FINEST <u>FULL-FOCUS</u> PICTURE

Zenith is proud to announce the world's finest *full-focus* picture, the long-time dream of TV science. Stays *entirely* in focus—automatically *locked* in focus. Zenith's new "Electronex" tube ends blur, distortion and edge-fading—brings you the superb picture quality and clarity you have dreamed of seeing in TV.

And in this TV-radio-phonograph combination, only Zenith gives you Cobra-Matic, simplest automatic record-player ever invented. Plays *any* size record, *any* speed now here or yet to come between 10 and 85 r.p.m., including

the new 16 r.p.m. All this plus Zenith Long-Distance AM and Super-Sensitive FM radio. Ask your Zenith dealer for a demonstration.

Only Zenith Television Has All This!

Provision for UHF. Simple insertion of tuner strips takes 15 minutes. • *New Distance-Reception.* Zenith's exclusive Fringe-Lock permanently holds finest pictures ever seen, even in weak or outlying signal areas. • *Minimum Reflection.* Tilted face-plate and wide-angle frame assure a perfect picture. • *Simple Automatic Tuning.* One-knob automatic Turret Tuner brings in picture and sound at one simple twist. • *Custom-Tuned Just for You!* When set is installed, the Zenith Turret Tuner is custom-tuned for peak performance in your home.

Shown Above . . . New Zenith "Barrie"
TV-Radio-Phonograph Console
Model J3069E. 17-inch (146 sq. in.) "Electronex" Tube screen. Cobra-Matic® record-player. FM-AM radio. The Modern motif superbly expressed in Gold Coast Afara specially selected.

Also makers of Zenith "Royal" and "Super Royal" Hearing Aids. Small, compact, beautifully designed. Money back guarantee. Sold only through authorized dealers at $75.

New Zenith "Kipling" TV-Radio-Phonograph Console. Model J2868R. 17-inch (146 sq. in.) "Electronex" Tube screen. Cobra-Matic® record-player. FM-AM radio. Beautiful Sheraton cabinet of Mahogany veneer.

Zenith Radio Corporation, Chicago 39, Illinois

First home television camera, RCA's "TV Eye," connects to any TV set—lets you watch children in the nursery or at play.

RCA "TV Eye" gives schools a private TV network, takes talks and demonstrations to classrooms.

In a railroad yard, RCA vidicon camera lets employees check car numbers at long range.

RCA vidicon camera in a bank, lets tellers verify signatures by television.

Tireless "TV Eye"

New RCA TV camera an alert watchman for home, school, industry

Based on the vidicon tube, developed by RCA, a versatile new instrument is on the way for homes, business, and schools—the RCA "TV Eye."

Light, compact, and easy to use, the RCA "TV Eye" is a camera unit which can be connected to standard home television receivers—makes any of the 23 million TV sets now in use a potential closed-circuit television system.

RCA's industrial version of the vidicon camera has already proved its place as an observer and guardian in science, industry, transportation, business—with new uses still being explored. Wherever distance or danger preclude a human observer's presence, the RCA vidicon camera can take his place to stand watch.

"TV Eye" plugs easily into standard TV sets. You just switch to the selected channel, and see everything that the camera sees.

RCA RADIO CORPORATION OF AMERICA
World leader in radio—first in television

There are Some Things
a Son or Daughter <u>won't</u> tell you!

"AW GEE, pop, why can't *we* get a television set?" You've heard that. But there's more you won't hear. *Do you expect a seven-year-old to find words for the deep loneliness he's feeling?*

He may complain—"The kids were mean and wouldn't play with me!" Do you expect him to blurt out the truth—that he's really ashamed to be with the gang—*that he feels left out because he doesn't see the television shows they see, know the things they know?*

You can tell someone about a bruised finger. How can a little girl describe a bruise deep inside? *No, your daughter won't ever tell you the humiliation she's felt in begging those precious hours of television from a neighbor.*

You give your child's *body* all the sunshine and fresh air and vitamins you can. *How about sunshine for his morale? How about vitamins for his mind?* Educators agree—television is all that and more for a growing child.

When television means so much more to a child than entertainment alone, can you deny it to your family any longer?

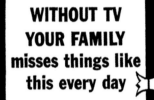

WITHOUT TV YOUR FAMILY misses things like this every day

TELEVISION is moving faster than you think. New programs, new stars make their debut every week. The longer you wait, the more you miss! Here's just a partial list.

A NEW KIND OF NEWS—You can actually see history made right before your eyes. Children in TV homes are more alert, better informed, often get high marks at school.

DRAMA for young and old—The brightest stars of the theatre now perform to millions—bring the great plays of all time to audiences who never before could see them.

CHILD PERFORMERS—Talented singers, dancers, musicians inspire your own children to learn faster, practice longer, willingly cultivate their own talents.

WORLD'S GREATEST athletic events—Fathers and sons follow their favorite teams together from a front row seat. Television helps teach your children sportsmanship.

THE WONDERFUL world of make believe—Experts say every child needs it as part of his normal development. And it makes mother's life a lot easier—especially on rainy days.

MUSIC DELUXE! Now you can *see* as well as hear your favorite orchestras, singers, instrumentalists! Yes, Television gets you right "on stage" seats, no money could buy!

LAUGHTER under your roof—the shared pleasure that binds your family closer. The greatest comedians of the entertainment world are in your living room every night on TV.

Angelo Patri
Noted Behaviorist and Authority on Child Guidance says:

"Youngsters today need television for their morale as much as they need fresh air and sunshine for their health. Social competence is a big force in any child's life. With it he can battle triumphantly for his place among his fellows.

"It is practically impossible for boys and girls to 'hold their own' with friends and schoolmates unless television is available to them. Of course there would be no conflict if parents brought television into the home. It would eliminate a situation that could cause great embarrassment to children. To have television is to be 'cock o' the walk. Not to have it, well, that is unthinkable."

Angelo Patri

TELEVISION
may never again cost so little!

EASY PAYMENTS—SEE YOUR DEALER TODAY

Top: Picture tubes being placed into carriage before being rolled into chamber. Right: Operator admitting compressed air into chamber.

The Torture Chamber
that tests the strength of RCA Picture Tubes

How *strong* is a picture tube? Well, certainly no stronger than its envelope. And that means that poor sealing of glass-to-glass or glass-to-metal, improper annealing of the glass—and even thermal or physical shock during manufacture—can contribute to structural weakness.

How *strong* should a picture tube be? Obviously, it must at least have adequate strength to be handled, transported, and installed safely. To insure safety, RCA has established a rigid standard of strength based on air-pressure tests evolved through unequaled years of experience.

Throughout the day, glass and metal picture tubes of each size are picked at random from the production lines, and placed in an air-compression chamber where they are subjected to "torturing" pressure for several minutes. Any tubes failing this test are examined by RCA production inspectors who can trace the fault and correct it on the production line almost as soon as it appears. Result ... *structurally weak tubes never reach your shop.*

RCA's constant vigilance at *all* stages of manufacture is your assurance that only top-quality RCA picture tubes leave the factory. In this way, RCA closely guards its own reputation ... *and yours as well.*

With RCA Receiving Tubes, as well as RCA Kinescopes, TOP-QUALITY CONTROL makes the difference.

RADIO CORPORATION of AMERICA
ELECTRON TUBES   HARRISON, N.J.

Even under the most HUMID CONDITIONS

RAYTHEON PICTURE TUBES

are 100% efficient...

thanks to **Raytheon's** new

CORONA INHIBITOR

Ordinary picture tubes are adversely affected by humidity and wet weather — may lose up to 10% of their brightness on damp days. Not so Raytheon made Television Picture Tubes with new CORONA INHIBITOR.

This amazing Raytheon development puts a "raincoat" on Raytheon Picture Tubes, guarantees the same *clear picture* rain or shine. Exhaustive tests proved conclusively that even under a water spray on the high voltage contact, Raytheon made Tubes showed *no loss of brightness.*

Give your customers the tubes that give constant clarity no matter what the weather. Ask your Raytheon Tube Distributor for Raytheon Television Picture Tubes.

Right for Sight!

RAYTHEON
Excellence in Electronics

RAYTHEON MANUFACTURING COMPANY
Receiving Tube Division
Newton, Mass., Chicago, Ill., Atlanta, Ga., Los Angeles, Calif.
RECEIVING AND PICTURE TUBES • RELIABLE SUBMINIATURE AND MINIATURE TUBES • GERMANIUM DIODES AND TRANSISTORS • RADIAC TUBES • MICROWAVE TUBES

Admiral

THE CLEAREST PICTURE IN *Television*

When it comes to *complete* home entertainment, everyone thinks of Admiral. It's a fact! Admiral makes more television combinations than all other brands put together. See this exquisite **NEW** Admiral today and you'll quickly understand why. You'll see the sharpest, brightest, clearest picture in television . . . Admiral's famous triple-play automatic phonograph . . . the super-powered Dynamagic radio. All in an authentic 18th Century cabinet with generous record storage space . . . at a sensational low price confirming again Admiral's claim to the greatest values in television. Available with 17 or 21-inch picture screen.

ON TV: "Lights Out," NBC, Mon., 9 PM, EST . . . "Stop the Music," ABC, Thurs., 8 PM, EST.

Model 37K36 with *Seventeen inch Television screen*

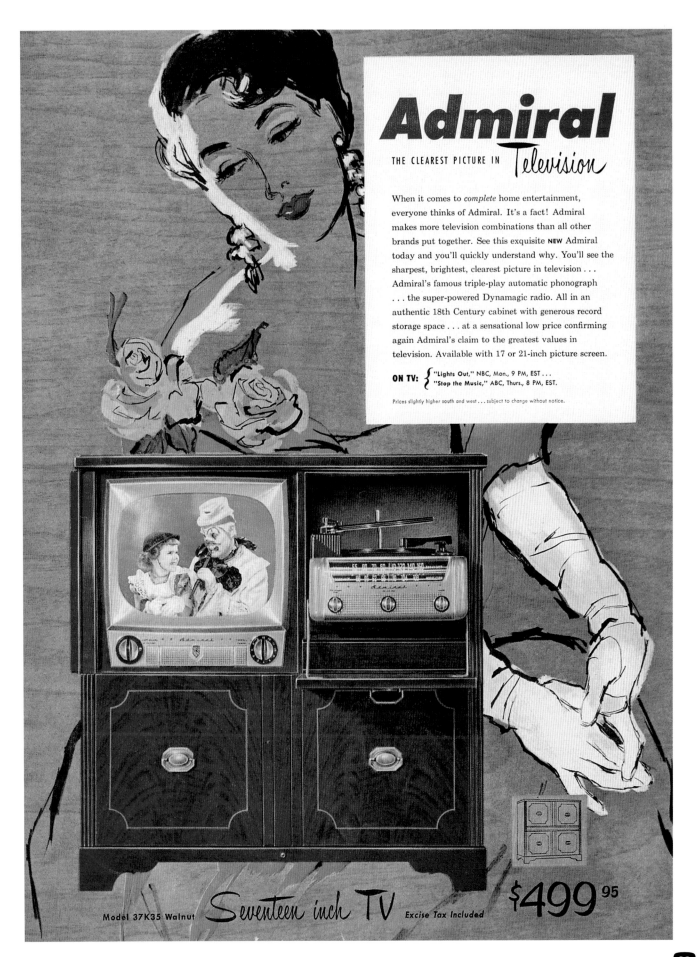

Admiral

THE CLEAREST PICTURE IN *Television*

When it comes to *complete* home entertainment, everyone thinks of Admiral. It's a fact! Admiral makes more television combinations than all other brands put together. See this exquisite **NEW** Admiral today and you'll quickly understand why. You'll see the sharpest, brightest, clearest picture in television . . . Admiral's famous triple-play automatic phonograph . . . the super-powered Dynamagic radio. All in an authentic 18th Century cabinet with generous record storage space . . . at a sensational low price confirming again Admiral's claim to the greatest values in television. Available with 17 or 21-inch picture screen.

ON TV: { "Lights Out," NBC, Mon., 9 PM, EST . . .
"Stop the Music," ABC, Thurs., 8 PM, EST.

Prices slightly higher south and west . . . subject to change without notice.

Model 37K35 Walnut *Seventeen inch* TV Excise Tax Included

$499⁹⁵

Admiral

THE CLEAREST PICTURE IN *Television*

Just remember this when choosing *your* television receiver: Admiral makes more television combinations than all other brands put together. You'll quickly understand why when you see the brilliant new 1951 models now on display at your Admiral dealer. You'll see the sharpest, brightest, clearest picture in television . . . Admiral's famous triple-play automatic phonograph with Dynamagic radio. A wide selection of modern and traditional cabinets with rectangular picture tubes ranging from 14″ to 20″ . . . priced as low as $349.95, excise tax included! The greatest values in complete home entertainment!

ON TV: "Lights Out," NBC, Mon., 9 PM, EST . . . "Stop the Music," ABC, Thurs., 8 PM, EST.

Model 321K18 with *Twenty inch Television screen*

Admiral

THE LUXURIOUS NEW *Tele-bar*

This is it . . . the ultimate in gracious living! Tele-bar, an exclusive Admiral creation, provides magnificent 20″ television, Dynamagic radio and triple-play automatic phonograph . . . combined with a luxurious built-in bar. Its exquisite liquor-proof cabinet provides a place for everything . . . stain-proof mixing tray, liquor-proof serving shelf, racks for glasses, storage space for bottles and "empties." Available in period mahogany, modern blond, and the new ultra-modern Silver Fox finish. See Tele-bar at your Admiral dealer, today!

ON TV: "Lights Out," NBC, Mon., 9 PM, EST
"Stop the Music," ABC, Thurs., 8 PM, EST.

So clear, so real you live the action

No streaks, no flutter, no flop-over will break the spell of television when you own a Westinghouse. You select your channel with a single dial, and electronic controls take over. Interference is caught and rejected by the exclusive Westinghouse Electronic Clarifier. Your clear picture stays clear. So, if you want television so real you live the action, buy a Westinghouse.

YOU CAN BE SURE...IF IT'S

Westinghouse

SALEM CHEST WITH 21-INCH PICTURE

This large-screen Westinghouse Salem Chest in satiny cherry and mahogany is a hand-crafted copy of a colonial masterpiece. It gives you famous Westinghouse Television performance. To receive UHF when it comes, you simply buy a tiny receptor you can plug in yourself. See the many fine Westinghouse sets at your dealer's now. Picture sizes range from 17" to 24", and prices start as low as $199.95 including Federal Tax and full-year picture tube warranty.

Enjoy TV's top dramatic show,
WESTINGHOUSE STUDIO ONE,
every week over CBS-TV

ADMIRAL 24″ TV $199⁹⁵*

with Smart Decorator-Styled Stand Free!
Save $57⁹⁵ while Limited Supply Lasts

FORMERLY $257⁹⁰*
NOW . . . $199⁹⁵*
SAVE $57⁹⁵

Just $30 extra with 82-Channel UHF

KING-SIZE TRADE-IN DURING 30-DAY SALE

The London—
mahogany finish

24″ TV Console—The London—in stunning contemporary cabinet with brass-tipped tapered legs. Right now your Admiral dealer will give you twice the usual trade-in on your old TV toward this magnificent set!

Think of it! You can own this striking ebony-finish 24″ Admiral TV—The Honduras —for less than many 21″ sets...complete with its matching decorator-styled stand! It's brand-new—factory-fresh—built just a few short weeks ago to sell for $239.95*, and the sturdy custom-built stand would regularly be $17.95 additional! It's your once-in-a-lifetime opportunity to own king-size 24″ TV at an unheard-of low price... so hurry, because quantities are strictly limited.

Your home deserves the best...that's always
(Choice of 5 Million TV owners)

Prices slightly higher South, West and Canada. Subject to change without notice.

the Chinese Classic by Stromberg-Carlson. Television-radio-phonograph. A complete home entertainment instrument
in a cabinet of incomparable beauty . . . hand-decorated by gifted artists against a rich background of red, green, ivory
or ebony lacquer—each an individual masterpiece, exclusively yours. For your relaxed hours of enjoyment, there is big-picture 19" television . . .
outstanding AM-FM radio . . . 3-speed record-player providing more than four hours of continuous music.
The longer you live with this fine instrument, the more convinced you'll be, "There is nothing finer than a Stromberg-Carlson."

"There is nothing finer than a
STROMBERG-CARLSON"®

Stromberg-Carlson television is priced from $289.95 to $975 including excise tax. (Slightly higher in South and West)

Now—television can be more to you than a picture. As the center of interest in your home, it can also be a thing of beauty, a constant tribute to your good taste. In this Stromberg-Carlson Classic superb performance in sight and sound is combined with a masterpiece of truly fine cabinetry. Here too, is exciting Panoramic Vision—which only Stromberg-Carlson can give you!

here is nothing finer than a STROMBERG-CARLSON."

The CLASSIC with exclusive PANORAMIC VISION has the widest viewing angle in 21 inch TV. Performance on UHF or VHF, even in fringe areas, is outstanding. Each cabinet is individually hand-decorated with authentic Chinese legend design on ivory, red, or ebony lacquer—and bears the artist's signature.

Stromberg-Carlson television is priced from $249.95 including excise tax and warranty. (Slightly higher in south and west). See classified pages of telephone book for nearby dealers.

The illustrations on these two pages and the two following appeared in a unique series of Sparton Television advertisements that ran in *Life* magazine in 1953. Sparton held a contest for its dealers to design window displays in their showrooms showcasing the manufacturer's sets. Winning contestants would not only have their window displays photographed for a Sparton ad, but also be credited, giving the proud dealer national exposure. The Sparton campaign also combined illustrators' renderings of whimsical locations for television sets; it's hard to tell the difference, in some cases, between the real and the imaginary settings due to the theatrical design and lighting that were used for the real locations to make them indistinguishable from the renderings. Locations of the real settings appear at the bottom of page 49.

Baseball Diamond (page 47), Higbee Company, Cleveland; Child's Western (upper left), Meier & Frank, Portland, Oregon; Child's Playland (lower left), Joslin's, Denver; Outer Space (upper right), Dayton Company, Minneapolis; Coronation of Queen Elizabeth— a major news event that year (lower right), Wanamaker's, New York City.

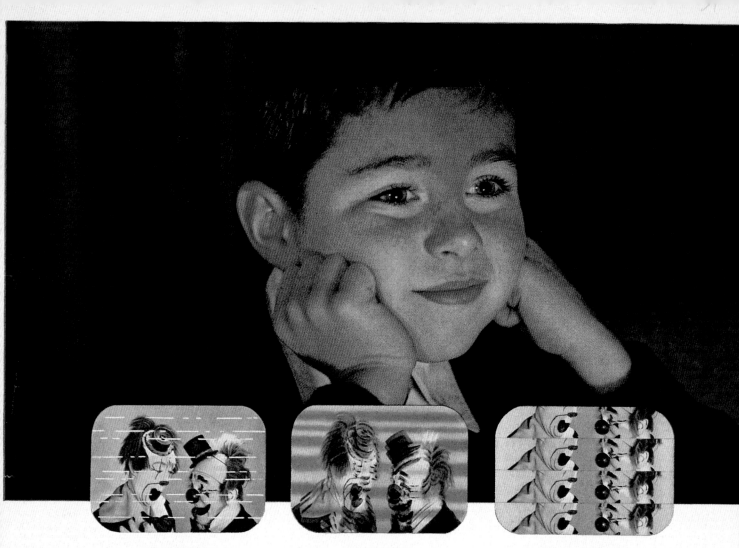

NO STREAKS   **NO FLUTTER**   **NO FLOPOVER**

Nothing to break the spell

NEW WESTINGHOUSE HI-VALUE TV GIVES YOU GREATEST EYE COMFORT

Sit back and watch your favorite TV shows with uninterrupted enjoyment. No annoying streaks, flutter, flopover every time a truck or automobile goes by, or a plane passes overhead! New 5-stage Electronic Clarifier—a Westinghouse exclusive—traps the 101 causes of interference and gives you pictures that start clear, stay clear *automatically*.

It's TV's most famous feature. Yet new Westinghouse with Electronic Clarifier

... True Dimension Picture ... new 100-mile-plus Tuner ... exclusive Automatic Area Selector ... sensational new styling ... Eye Comfort Mask ... and UHF-VHF tuning on single dial ... costs no more than ordinary TV. At the lowest prices you've ever seen, they're today's biggest TV values.

... Westinghouse Electric Corporation, Television-Radio Division, Metuchen, N. J.

YOU CAN BE SURE...IF IT'S
Westinghouse

Delight to eye and ear! Handsome 21-inch console finely crafted in rich mahogany (Model 830K21), at new low prices.

BE SURE TO TUNE IN EVERY WEEK...TV's TOP DRAMATIC SHOW: WESTINGHOUSE STUDIO ONE

A fresh new look
in TV design ...
WESTINGHOUSE CAPRI

Here's TV keyed to today's living and newest fashions in home furnishings! It's the new 1954 Capri, created for Westinghouse by Harley Earl, famous luxury car designer. The Capri series combines good looks with down-to-earth usefulness and unmatched performance.

Styled to fit any decorating scheme, Capri is equally smart without the base as a stunning, economical table model, or with the base as a perfectly matched ensemble. The new height and off-white picture mask assure greatest eye comfort. Cabinet is stain-resistant, easy to keep clean. Contemporary colors are decorator favorites, gray linen stripe with contrasting walnut-finish base, mahogany finish with matching base, or bisque on walnut-finish, model 827T21, (above). Built-in UHF/VHF antenna. UHF optional, at extra cost.

See your Westinghouse dealer *today*. See the complete selection of new 1954 Westinghouse television sets—famous for No Streaks, No Flutter, No Flopover—*now* at new low prices.

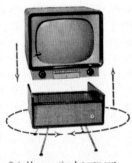

Swivel base—optional at extra cost —adjusts for easy viewing from anywhere in room. Speaker may be easily moved from set to base for even richer sound fidelity. Westinghouse Electric Corp., TV-Radio Division, Metuchen, N. J.

YOU CAN BE SURE...IF IT'S Westinghouse

TUNE IN EVERY WEEK...TV'S TOP DRAMATIC SHOW...WESTINGHOUSE STUDIO ONE

EVEN BLINDFOLDED...YOU GET PERFECT TUNING

WESTINGHOUSE AUTOMATIC TUNING 7

No more tuning...
New Westinghouse TV
does it for you!

EVEN BLINDFOLDED...YOU GET PERFECT TUNING

WESTINGHOUSE AUTOMATIC TUNING 7

52

EVEN BLINDFOLDED YOU GET PERFECT TUNING— AUTOMATICALLY!

EVEN BLINDFOLDED YOU GET PERFECT TUNING— AUTOMATICALLY!

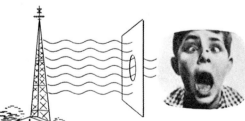

ORDINARY "NARROW BAND" SETS
simply *can't* reproduce full wide-band signal
FCC requires TV stations to send. Note blurry
detail. See harsh whites and blacks with few
"middle-tones" in-between.

WESTINGHOUSE "BROAD BAND" TV
is engineered to receive and reproduce *all* of
signal from the TV station. See needle-sharp
detail. Over entire picture, added "middle-
tones" give a new life-like realism.

New Westinghouse BROAD BAND TV gives you 22% MORE DETAIL!

Now, a TV set that's engineered to bring you ALL of the signal the TV station sends!

With wonderful Westinghouse "Broad Band" TV you see pictures that are breathtaking in their realism—pictures with *22% more* detail than sets not having this feature! Detail that's sharp instead of blurry. Tones that are beautifully modeled instead of harsh and contrasty. Images so life-like they bring new pleasure to your favorite TV shows!

But, that's only the beginning! 1957 Westinghouse TV gives you Push-Bar Power Tuning, Push Button On-Off switch. Automatic Gain Control that smooths out "flutter" from airplanes and street traffic. Silver Safeguard Chassis that gives you amazing new freedom from service calls . . . optional "Chairside" Remote Control . . . space-saving Slim-Trim styling.

Never has any set given so much for your money. Let your Westinghouse Dealer prove it to you *today!*

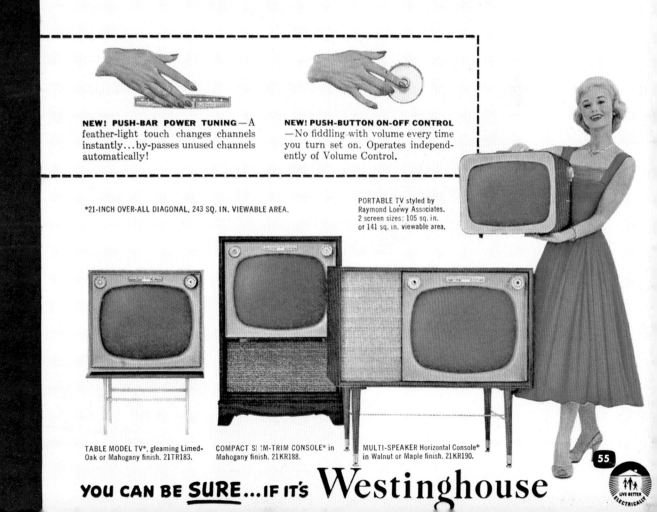

NEW! PUSH-BAR POWER TUNING—A feather-light touch changes channels instantly...by-passes unused channels automatically!

NEW! PUSH-BUTTON ON-OFF CONTROL—No fiddling with volume every time you turn set on. Operates independently of Volume Control.

*21-INCH OVER-ALL DIAGONAL, 243 SQ. IN. VIEWABLE AREA.

PORTABLE TV styled by Raymond Loewy Associates. 2 screen sizes: 105 sq. in. or 141 sq. in. viewable area.

TABLE MODEL TV*, gleaming Limed-Oak or Mahogany finish. 21TR183.

COMPACT SLIM-TRIM CONSOLE* in Mahogany finish. 21KR188.

MULTI-SPEAKER Horizontal Console* in Walnut or Maple finish. 21KR190.

55

YOU CAN BE _SURE_...IF IT'S Westinghouse

LIVE BETTER ELECTRICALLY

RCA Victor jet-tested portable TV prove

In test* by Boeing engineers RCA Victor portable brings in mirror-sharp picture 35,000 feet up! *Think what it can do in your home!*
Even in distant and difficult reception areas these new transformer-powered portables perform beautifully. Trim, tapered, compact, they even *look* powerful. Yet they're ever so easy to carry—*really* portable. For all its sky-high power, new RCA Victor jet-tested portable TV carries down-to-earth prices. Your RCA Victor dealer has just the size and color you want. Make your choice soon.

 **RCA VICTOR** RADIO CORPORATION OF AMERICA

56

Easy-going jet styling, sky-high power. *Townsman,* 108 sq. in. picture (14PT9 $139.95. *Dorsey,* 156 sq. in. picture (17PT904) $169.95. Also shown, at top, le right: *Tarrytown,* 262 sq. in. picture (21PT909) $229.95. *Sophisticate,* 156 in. picture (17PD907) $199.95. *Urbanite,* 108 sq. in. picture (14PD903) $159

ower in new Boeing 707 jetliner at 600 mph!

ew kind of luxury awaits you in the Boeing jet airliners. New spaciousness new beauty everywhere. Not far from your **roo**my chair there's the charm of y lounge—where you can enjoy congenial company. You'll be delighted with colors, new designs, attractive new arrangements and many novel conveniences.

In a few months, *you* will be able to enjoy jet-age travel aboard the superb Boeing 707. What will be different about travel in a Boeing jet airliner? Almost everything. Your route is a cloudless skyway far above the weather. There is no noise, no engine vibration. You discover new freedom in spacious cabins and lounges. Then, in half the conventional flight time, you arrive—as sparkling as when you walked on board. You've discovered a wonderful new way to travel—on jetliners by Boeing, world's most experienced builder of multi-engine jet aircraft.

These airlines will fly Boeing 707 and shorter-range 720 jet airliners:

AIR FRANCE • AIR-INDIA INTERNATIONAL • AMERICAN AIRLINES • BRANIFF INTERNATIONAL AIRWAYS • BRITISH OVERSEAS AIRWAYS CORPORATION • CONTINENTAL AIR LINES • CUBANA DE AVIACION • LUFTHANSA GERMAN AIRLINES PAN AMERICAN WORLD AIRWAYS • QANTAS EMPIRE AIRWAYS • SABENA BELGIAN WORLD AIRLINES • SOUTH AFRICAN AIRWAYS • TRANS WORLD AIRLINES • UNITED AIR LINES • VARIG AIRLINES OF BRAZIL

BOEING 707 and 720

57

TOMORROW IS HERE!

General Electric begins a whole new trend in television styling with the "Designer Series"

Never before now—sets designed like this! Trim, slim and graceful, the cabinets look less than handspan deep. The "Designers" *belong beautifully* in any room.

And what's more, you can carry them from room to room—they have recessed handles to make it easy.

But that's not all! *They perform like consoles!* Because they're built like con-soles—each packs a high-powered chassis, a power transformer.

And what sound—marvelously clear, lifelike! Built-in telescoping antennas, too. Colors? Choice of 5—fresh, lively, light-hearted as Spring! Prices? Irresistible.

Don't wait! Be the first to own a "De-signer." Years from now it'll still be ahead of its time!

"Barclay 21" above—21" overall diagonal measurement—262 sq. inches of picture area.

"Gramercy 17"—17" overall diagonal measurement—155 square inches of picture area.

Progress Is Our Most Important Product

GENERAL ⬡ ELECTRIC

THE LOOK OF THE SIXTIES !

"FORECASTER"

The "Forecaster" captures the modern mood with dynamic contrast of materials—genuine mahogany veneers and antique white, accented with a bright metallic finish.

You'll be delighted, too, at the big-set performance of this table model. It has a console chassis, full-power transformer, front-mounted speaker, stereo-phono jacks and 21-inch screen with dark safety-window for sharp contrast in all 262 square inches of picture area.

All of this happily combines to make the "Forecaster" the set that's ahead of its time in styling, picture and sound. You'll really get excited when you see it for yourself at your General Electric dealer's.

GENERAL ELECTRIC

Noted western illustrator Charles Schridde created this illustration of the man and woman watching television in their treehouse for a Motorola ad. The public response was so great that Motorola asked Schridde (even after he left the ad agency that Motorola had hired) to continue with a series of similar illustrations for its home electronics advertisements, which ran in *Life* magazine and *The Saturday Evening Post* from 1961 to 1963 (pages 60–65).

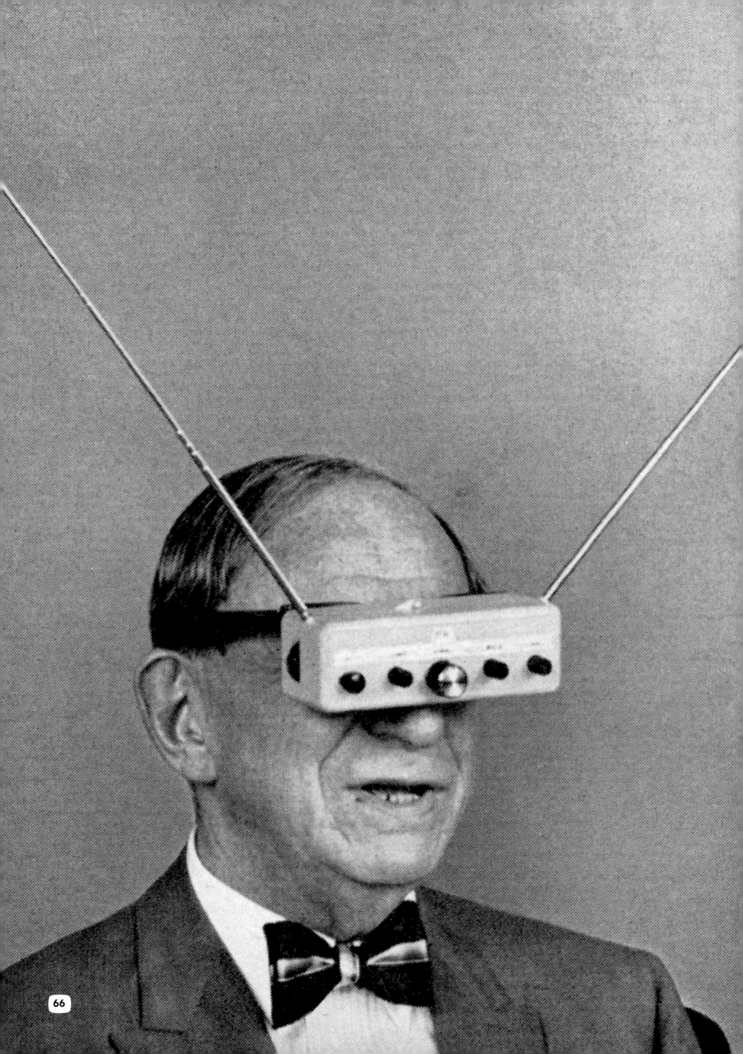

3

All I Want for Christmas Is . . .

All I Want for Christmas Is . . .

Manufacturers' television set print ads appeared in great numbers every fall, from 1947 through the color boom of the mid- to late 1960s. These ads were launched in connection with the start of each new television season, as well as with Christmas, a time when consumers were most easily persuaded to buy sets. In most of the Christmas ads Santa appears on-screen to remind fathers that a television set is the gift that keeps on giving. Artist Norman Rockwell, who earlier had painted the installation of a television antenna on a residential roof for a postwar *Saturday Evening Post* cover, was drafted in the early 1950s to render two Christmas ads for DuMont. In the 1952 illustration, children and their parents appear more enthused over their new DuMont than they ever would have been had visions of sugar plums started dancing in their heads. In the 1950 ad two children and a black cocker spaniel appear less than sanguine, possibly because they are disappointed that their father purchased their set too late to be delivered before Christmas. Or could it be that the set sits just outside the illustration, and the kids and their canine are simply . . . spellbound? The most famous (and collector-desirable) holiday television set ad is arguably the best of them all: RCA's 1955 "White Christmas" ad, monochromatic except for the flesh tones in its models' faces and hands and, most prominently, the color on the television screen and the set's cabinet.

All is clear...
all is bright

✦ The time for candlelight and carols and children gathered
round your feet . . . for the warm heart and the joyous
reunion with those long missed at home . . . for the yule log, the
fragrant balsam, and all good things that bind families and
friends closer together. One of these is television. This
Christmas the magic window of G-E Black-Daylite Television
will remind millions that no other gift gives so much.

General Electric Company, Electronics Park, Syracuse, N. Y.

You can put your confidence in —

GENERAL ⒼⒺ ELECTRIC

The Present with a Future...

THE WESTMINSTER SERIES II BY DU MONT
19-inch Lifetone* television.
Built-in radio—both standard AM and
static-free FM. Automatic 3-speed phonograph.
Professional quality tape recorder.
High fidelity sound system with three speakers.
Automatic time-clock control mechanism.
*Trade Mark

TELEVISION, as we know it, began with Dr. Du Mont. In his laboratory the cathode ray tube developed from a scientific curiosity to the practical picture tube that now is television's heart. Many such electronic developments mark the path of Du Mont pioneering. Du Mont gave you the first home television sets—the first television network—the first Life-Size television. Today Du Mont continues to give you the newest and best in television—big 17- and 19-inch telepictures, fine furniture craftsmanship, all the built-in values that mean lasting enjoyment for you.

1951 DuMont television

THE REVERE BY DuMon[t]
*17-inch Rectangular picture. Buil[t]
radio. Plug-in for record pla[yer]*

THE CARLTON BY DuMo[nt]
*17-inch Rectangular picture. Pl[ug-in]
record player.*

THE BURLINGAME BY DuM[ont]
*17-inch Rectangular picture. Buil[t]
radio. Plug-in for record play[er]*

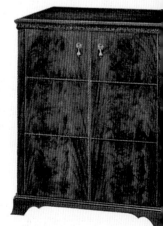

THE MOUNT VERNON BY DuM[ont]
*19-inch pictures. Built-in FM
Plug-in for record player.*

No less than wonderful!

Here is DuMont's most advanced thinking . . .

[b]rilliantly designed, built with craftsman's pride,

and engineered to give you

better, longer-lived performance.

First with the finest in Television

Enchanted lands...right in your home

No dreamed-of magic carpet ever journeyed through more wonderful realms...
or traveled so far so fast. There's a world of inspiration in television.
And the set you honor with a place in your family circle should be fine indeed ... an instrument
built with pride to be owned with pride. The new Du Mont television receivers,
in hand-crafted cabinets, incorporate the latest Du Mont electronic advances
from the laboratories that introduced television to America. They offer you the ultimate
in television enjoyment. A complete line of consoles, combinations, table models.

DU MONT

First with the finest in Television

THE WESTMINSTER SERIES II BY DU MONT
19-inch Lifetone* picture. Built-in AM-FM radio.
Automatic time clock control.
Automatic 3-speed phonograph. Tape recorder.
Cabinet designed by Herbert Rosengren.

* Trade Mark   Copyright 1950, Allen B. Du Mont Laboratories, Inc., Television Receiver Division, East Paterson, N. J., and the Du Mont Television Network, 515 Madison Ave., New York 22, N.Y.

A Merrier Christmas...
through DuMont *Research!*

Norman Rockwell

This year, television brings a merrier Christmas to more families than ever before. It holds forth
a promise of better living and greater understanding throughout the world.
DuMont is proud of the part it has played in the growth of the television industry...
an industry founded on Dr. DuMont's development of the cathode-ray tube.
In the future many young men will find DuMont is the company where they may best realize their ambitions
in the field of electronics. And DuMont will continue to give America more of the wonders of life
yet hidden in this electronic age.

DuMont

first with the finest in Television and Electronics

here's the GIFT that sings, talks and lives for years..

No gift ever so completely matched the spirit of Christmas as the miraculous MOTOROLA table model VT71 TELEVISION receiver. Here is the wonder of wonders! News, sports, drama, comedy... in your living room as it happens...with famous people in famous places! The Motorola Golden View picture is star bright, crisp and sharp! The receiver is so light (26½ lbs.) you can move it from room to room and installation is quick and easy. You can have it in time for the big Christmas Holiday programs, and at a price all can afford. **$189 95***

Federal Excise Tax $1.30

Table Radio-Phonograph. "Floating Action" changer handles ten 10" or eight 12" records. Model 68F11

Thrilling Beauty, Low Price. New table radio in six decorator colors. Powerful... rich tone. Model 58R11

Playmate Jr. Tiny...light ...powerful...wonderful tone! AC/DC, Battery (batteries extra). Model 5A7A

6-in-1 Console. Television, Automatic Phonograph for standard (or Long Playing) records. FM-AM radio plus record storage. Model VF103

Gorgeous Table Model. Shows constant, crystal-clear pictures. Hand-rubbed Furniture Styled cabinet. Model VT105

Motorola
TELEVISION and GIFT RADIOS

MOTOROLA INC. • CHICAGO 51, ILLINOIS

Prices slightly higher in south and west. Installation extra on all television receivers. See Your Classified Phone Book for name of nearest Motorola Dealer. Prices subject to change without notice.

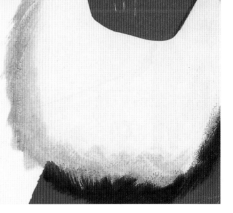

 DAYLIGHT TELEVISION
80% BRIGHTER

The whole family will love This gift

G-E TELEVISION—BIGGEST VALUE YET!
Great new Automatic Sound. Just tune the best picture,
the sound is right every time! Bigger-than-ever picture on a
10" conventional tube! Compact rosewood plastic cabinet.
Model 10T1 is *all* television! **$199.95***
*Plus tax, installation. Prices slightly higher West and South—
subject to change without notice.

What a wonderful experience, with the magic of television added to the magic of Christmas! G-E Daylight Television will bring your family Christmas joy *the whole year 'round!* It's now finer than ever with great new Automatic Sound. *The best picture automatically brings you the best sound,* even in fringe areas! You don't have to re-tune sound when changing channels. There is never any drift effect, and you can actually tune out many local picture interferences! All this, plus greater eye comfort. G-E Daylight Television, 80% brighter than ordinary television under the same conditions, can be viewed in a fully lighted room as eye specialists recommend! You'll find a wide selection of consoles and table models, all popular-priced. Look at Model 12C 105 with its built-in antenna. Big 12½" tube. Genuine mahogany veneered cabinet. For a merrier Christmas, put a G-E under the tree!

General Electric Company, Electronics Park, Syracuse, New York
See and hear the General Electric Fred Waring show on television — CBS-TV network, Sundays, 9 P M, EST

You can put your confidence in —

GENERAL ⓖⓔ ELECTRIC

Give your family a new thrill this Christmas morning
Motorola TV

16 inch TV combination FM/AM radio
—3-speed phonograph. In mahogany
or limed oak. **Model 17F1**

Put yourself in this picture by telling your dealer to deliver a Motorola in time for Christmas. Motorola has all the features you want—big, bright pictures—easy operation (just 2 simple controls)—and trouble-free performance (we actually play it at the factory to make sure it works when you get it).

Take your choice of a swell selection of Fashion Award table models, consoles and phonograph combinations—screen sizes from 14 to 20 inches. 29 models, all priced to fit your pocketbook. There's a Motorola for *your* home—*your* budget—*your* family this Christmas. See your Motorola dealer soon.

See your classified directory for the name of your nearest Motorola dealer. Specifications subject to change without notice.

GIVE A MOTOROLA AND YOU KNOW YOU GIVE THE BEST

Admiral Triple Thrill—

Complete
HOME ENTERTAINMENT
ALL IN *One*
LUXURIOUS CONSOLE
$549⁵⁰
WALNUT

FM-AM RADIO

2-SPEED PHONOGRAPH

MAGIC MIRROR TELEVISION

From Admiral . . . comes this triple thrill in complete home entertainment. **MAGIC MIRROR TELEVISION** brings you steady, mirror-clear pictures on a big 10″ direct-view screen . . . the clearest pictures of them all! Super-powered by 29 tubes (including rectifiers) to assure dependable performance even in outlying areas. Complete channel coverage. Here, too, is a powerful **FM-AM RADIO** including the finest features in static-free FM as engineered by Admiral. New **2-SPEED AUTOMATIC PHONOGRAPH** plays standard as well as the sensational new L.P. (long play) "microgroove" records. Imagine! 45 minutes of music . . . equivalent to a standard 6-record album . . . all from a single 12″ record. Truly a triple-thrill . . . all combined in a breathtakingly beautiful cabinet only 48 inches wide! See it! Hear it! Today!

Admiral "5 Star Revue" on Television! NBC Network, Sundays, 7:30 p.m., EST

AMERICA'S SMART SET *Admiral*

80

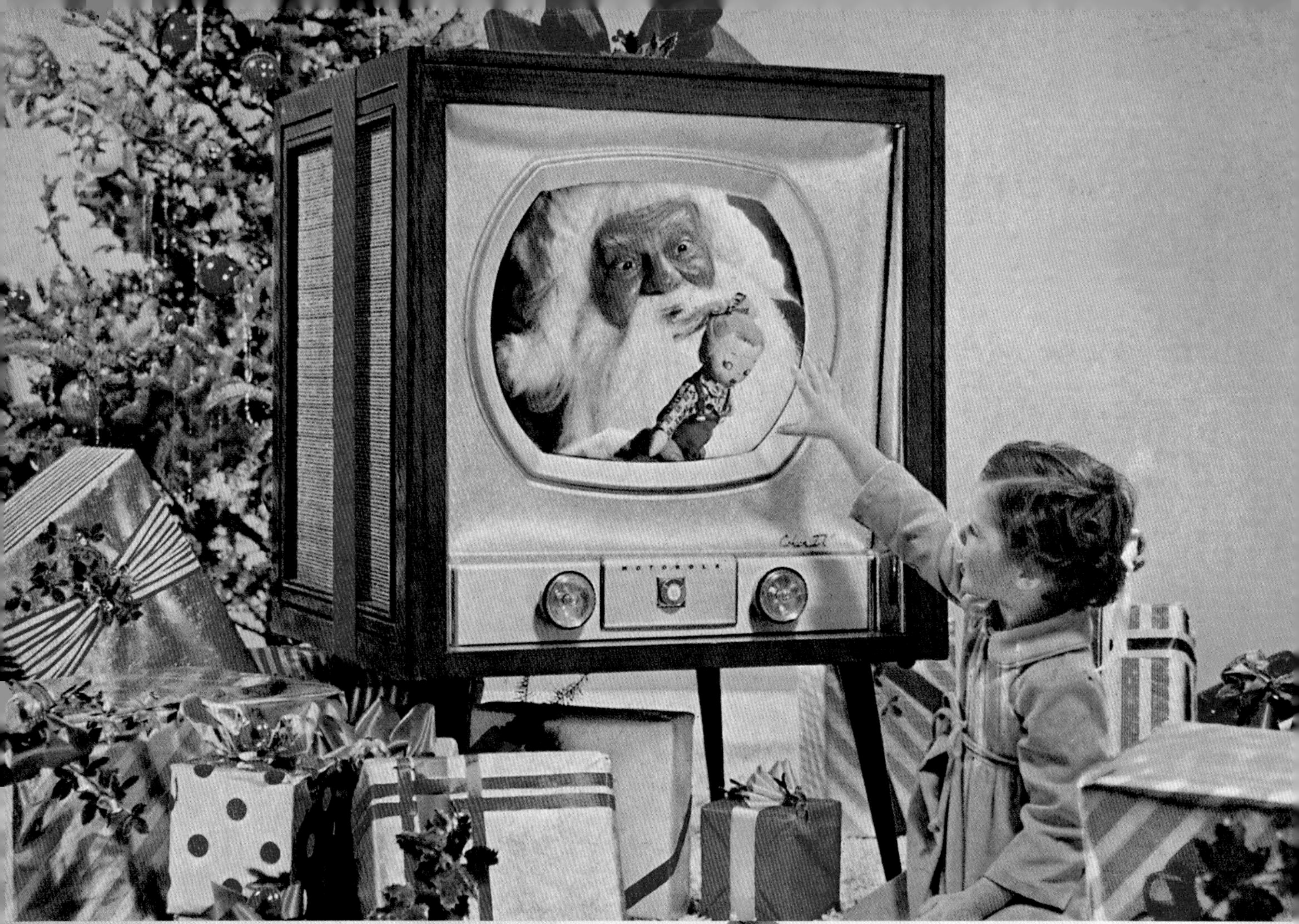

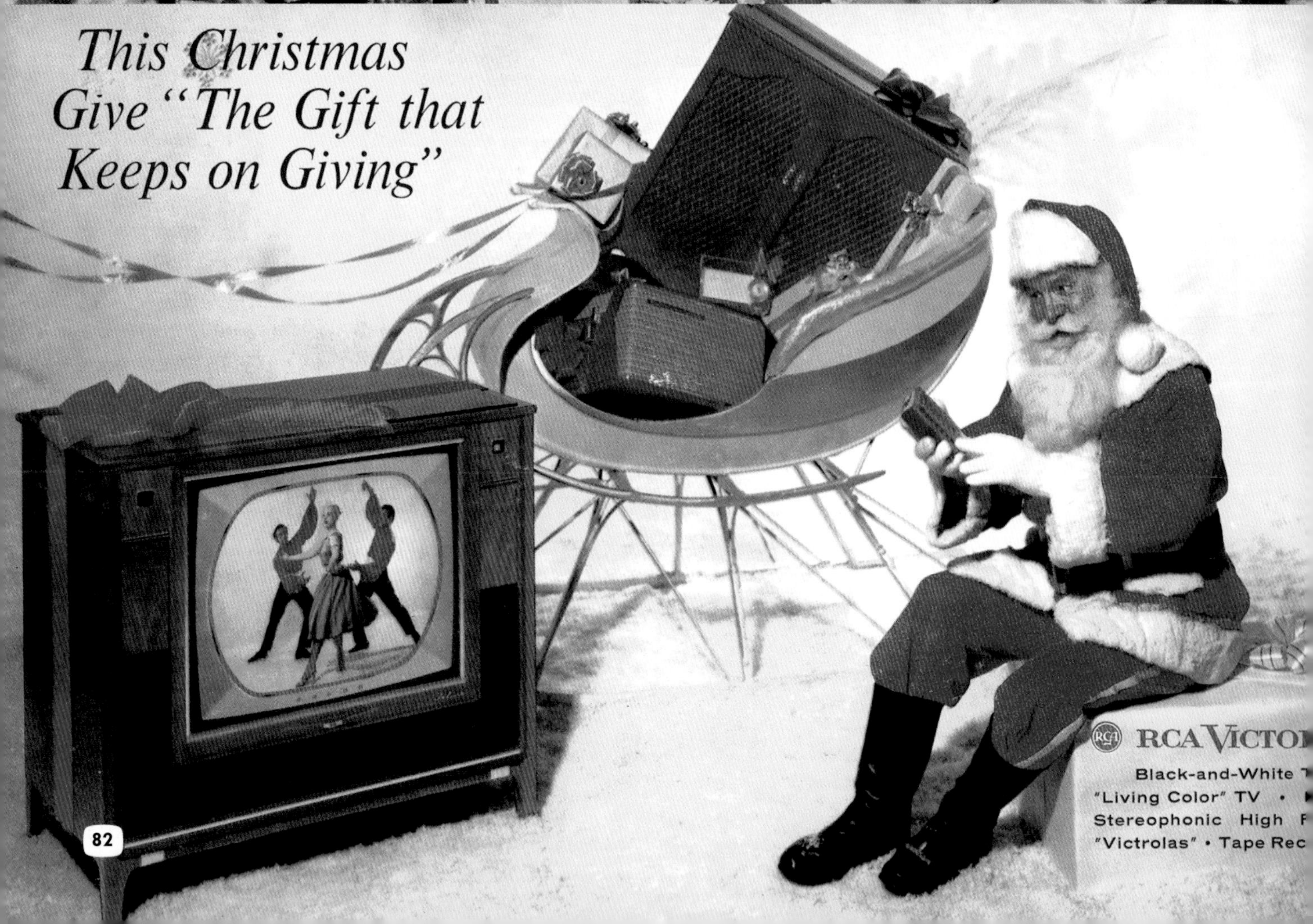

This Christmas
Give "The Gift that
Keeps on Giving"
RCA VICTO
Black-and-White T
"Living Color" TV •
Stereophonic High F
"Victrolas" • Tape Rec

New Director 21. Big Color Television console with two speakers. Mahogany finish. Also in blond tropical hardwood finish (21CT662), $895. Not shown: New Seville 21. (21CT661) $795.

BIG COLOR BY RCA VICTOR

This Christmas give your family the wonderful world of color! For Big Color TV is here—in two beautiful new 21-inch color sets by RCA Victor.

Christmas morning . . . The whole family rushes into the living room. Right there, next to the Christmas tree, is your gift to them — a new RCA Victor TV set! You wait for just the right moment . . . turn it on . . . and watch Color come into their lives.

Eyes widen . . . faces light up. And no wonder —for this is new, exciting 21-inch *Color* Television by RCA Victor!

The year around—day and night—they'll enjoy

the wonders of Color TV. Spectacular musicals, children's programs, sports events, drama — all alive with *Color!*

Of course, because RCA pioneered and developed Compatible Color, the same set brings you all your favorite black-and-white programs in black-and-white, too.

So visit your RCA Victor dealer this week. There's still time to give your family the *nicest* Christmas gift—Big Color by RCA Victor!

WORRY-FREE! With an RCA Victor Factory Service Contract (optional, extra), your Color TV set is installed and serviced by RCA's own technicians. Only RCA Victor TV owners can buy this Contract.

See Milton Berle, Martha Raye alternately on NBC-TV, on 2 out of every 3 Tuesdays. And don't miss NBC-TV's spectacular "Producers' Showcase" in RCA Compatible Color or black-and-white, Monday, Dec. 12.

Manufacturer's nationally advertised UHF-VHF list prices shown, subject to change.

FIRST IN BLACK-AND-WHITE TELEVISION

RCA VICTOR
Tmks ® RADIO CORPORATION OF AMERICA

FIRST IN COMPATIBLE COLOR TELEVISION

4

TELEVISION BLAZON –
Color in a Black-and-White World

TELEVISION BLAZON –
Color in a Black-and-White World

Color bigger than life! How do you re-create the color television experience in a print ad? That was the question that faced advertisers in the spring of 1954 as the first all-electronic color sets began to roll off assembly lines. The obvious answer would seem to be to shoot a color photograph of the color picture on the television screen. But due to the lower resolution of the television screen when compared to the higher one used in print photography, this would have resulted in "muddy" photos and hurt sales. Instead, ad agencies adopted a two-pronged approach: focus on comparisons with black-and-white television, and tap into the kind of positive emotional response one might experience upon seeing color television for the first time.

Comparison ads showed a portion of the picture on the screen in black and white (as most people experienced television at the time) with a crucial section of the photo in color: a dancer singled out in a chorus line, half of Fred Astaire, three-quarters of the *Bonanza* cast, and so on. RCA/NBC's agency expanded this campaign by using multiple-page ads for increased dramatic effect. For example, a reader saw entertainer Maurice Chevalier in black and white on the right page of *Colliers,* only to turn and find the same photo of Chevalier on the left page, but in *color.*

By 1956, *Colliers* was in its death throes (in part due to the public's abandonment of print media for television), and RCA and NBC used their increased color television advertising budgets to run as many ads as possible from April to December 1956 before the magazine's demise in January 1957. Where in previous years they might not have run a single color television ad in any of the high-circulation weeklies for months, they now placed two in the same April 27, 1956, issue of *Colliers.* Of all the week-

lies, *Colliers* used the highest-quality paper and color printing process. Even fifty years later it is hard to find fading, yellowing, or crumbling pages in an intact issue. NBC and RCA used *Colliers'* color printing to good effect. One comparison ad shows, on one page, black-and-white television's harsh, reflected light on viewers' faces, with the following page showing the same group now basking in the warm, almost fireplace-like glow of RCA's color set. The comparison ads in *Colliers* reached their pinnacle with the six-page spread in April 1956 featuring ice skater/movie star Sonja Henie. Even still, the most clever comparison ad of all appeared not in *Colliers,* but in *TV Guide.*

In *TV Guide's* October 18, 1958, issue, RCA/NBC ran another six-page ad. But this time, readers were instructed to pull out a two-page, color spread of George Gobel sitting on a studio floor with the bottom halves of beautifully gowned chorines. Readers were to hold it up to the bottom half of their black-and-white sets when an on-air signal was given during the October 21 broadcast of Gobel's variety show. This setup required Gobel and the women to strike a rehearsed pose and hold it for a full minute so that viewers could make the comparison—which, it must be noted, was *not* between an RCA color set and viewers' black-and-white pictures, but between viewers' pictures and the higher-definition color ad. It may have been misleading, but it was inspired. The ad also asked viewers to tune their AM radios to their local NBC station and place them to the right of their television sets to create true stereo for the broadcast. Imagine, both color and stereo television where none had existed moments before! How many HDTV sets might dealers sell today if the public could sample a digital high-definition picture on an analog color set? Actually, the Gobel spread is more representative of today's printlike HDTV picture, and comparing it with an analog color set would be closer to the truth than it was between black-and-white and color television circa 1958.

TUESDAY NIGHT, OCTOBER 21, GEORGE GOBEL
PUTS YOU RIGHT IN THE ACT! ALL YOU NEED
IS YOUR TELEVISION SET AND YOUR RADIO

**THE NEXT FEW PAGES WILL SHOW YOU HOW
TO ENJOY ONE OF THE MOST REWARDING
HOURS IN ENTERTAINMENT HISTORY.**

YOU'LL HEAR HOW AMAZINGLY REAL

YOU'LL SEE THE DIFFERENCE COLOR TV MAKES!

your NBC **radio** station as well as on TV. Place the radio at least eight feet **to the right** of your TV set. What **you** hear will be dramatic stereophonic sound — sound with dimension and direction. You'll hear magnificent music, special effects and demonstrations of new stereophonic sound. For even more life-like stereo, listen to RCA Victor's brilliant "Living Stereo" recordings on a new Stereo-High Fidelity "Victrola."®

REO SOUND IS!

At some point during this special show, George Gobel will stop everything and hold a surprise scene in "stop motion" for a full minute. On the following pages, you will find an exact replica of **half** of this scene in glowing color. When George gives the signal, place this picture against the lower half of your black and white TV screen ... and see for yourself the wonderful warmth and realism color can add to TV viewing. **When George gives the word, pull this page gently to your left to release page from staples. Open out and there's your own Color TV demonstration page.**

WHEN GEORGE GIVES THE WORD ON TUESDAY NIGHT, PLACE THIS PICTURE

HE LOWER HALF OF YOUR TV SCREEN AND SEE THE DIFFERENCE COLOR MAKES!

A star today: Nanette Fabray ▶ poses prior to a 'spectacular.'

Test pattern' then: Nanette Fabray, aiding in RCA color experiments.

Test Pattern Makes Good

'COLORful' Describes Nanette's TV Career

A close-up made during the tests.

Few of the big-name stars in this season's TV color "spectaculars" have ever *seen* a color TV show, much less appeared in one. But Nanette Fabray, who is scheduled to star in an extravaganza for producer Max Liebman on NBC, was a color TV star way back in 1942. Probably the original live-test-pattern girl—on whom the cameramen train their lenses to make certain their colors are true— Nan has logged well over 1000 hours of color TV work.

Nan was an aspiring young musical comedy actress in 1942 when, from among a group of other young hopefuls, she was selected to star in a CBS color demonstration for the Federal Communications Commission.

"The CBS engineers had just solved the problem of how to present a moonlit scene in color," Nan recalls. "Naturally, that meant I did a song that had 'moonlit' in the title."

(In those days, programming boys

Continued on page 22

Make-up artists seek right color values.   Technician checks for proper lighting.

a camera artist makes

The First Color Commercial

COLOR television will brighten a lot of living rooms, but it's adding new furrows to the brows of the men who make TV commercials. Color multiplies the problems of costuming, staging, lighting and filming, although experts think it also will increase the sales impact.

Vienna-born Peter Elgar made the commercial shown in the accompanying pictures for the Pall Mall company. He believes it to be the first commercial made in color. It will be shown shortly on the first Pall Mall show to be color-cast, and also was photographed in black-and-white for immediate use.

Filming of the 60-second spot took 15 hours. Additional weeks were required to build the set, select the costumes and props, hire the technicians, choose and rehearse the six

actors. When Elgar couldn't find a harlequin outfit of the proper color, he had one hand-printed.

In the film, two masqueraders dance out on the terrace, they are serenaded by troubadours, then light cigarets of the proper brand and speak well of them in the brief sales message.

Elgar, now 49, made many educational and artistic films in Europe, including religious films for the Vatican. He never heard of a spot commercial until March of 1951, when he had just completed a sensitive film of a child learning to read, "The Impressionable Years," for the State Department. He went to an ad agency with an idea for some institutional films. They suggested the spots.

"It is like making any other motion picture," Elgar says, "except that the finished film is 60 seconds long."

Bennett Grant, left, and Alice Wallace, as masqueraders, take time for a smoke.   Elaborate setting and costumes produce the desired result—a lighted cigaret.

Then you turn the COLOR knob (the top one in row of small knobs in the control panel pictured on the opposite page) a half turn to the right or more to get the intensity of color you want. Then you turn the HUE knob (immediately below the COLOR knob) to obtain the correct colors. This is the one that can turn flesh red, green or whatever. When you've got a good, normal flesh tone, you may want to adjust the COLOR knob again to make the performers look paler or more flushed. That's all there is to it.

Lovely Marliss Johnson posed for our demonstration, and the set used was an RCA-Victor.

Too Purple, which means the HUE knob has been turned too far to the left. Turn it to right slowly until picture is normal.

Too Green. Note the flesh tones in contrast to the large normal picture on opposite page. Turn HUE knob to le

Too Little Color. Flesh tones look too pale. Turn the COLOR knob to the right until the condition is corrected.

Too Much Color. Marliss looks flushe This means the COLOR knob must turned to the left for color balanc

How To Tune A Color TV Set

Tuning a color set is just two knobs more difficult than tuning a standard black-and-white set. But it's much more fun. If you like, you can wind up with a green Red Skelton, a blue Red Barber or even a purple Red Buttons. To do the thing right, though, you first tune to get a good black-and-white picture.

Color — For Titles, Too

THEY NAME THE SHOW AND SET THE MOOD

When a show—regular or spectacular—is colorcast, multi-hued title cards are used to identify the program and establish mood. Although these cards are often on screen no more than five or ten seconds, artists get prices ranging from $25 (for lettering) to $3000.

Studio One plot was suggested in title card by Seymour Chwast.

Frank Aloise and Harvey Schmidt furnished set of 'Cyrano' cards.

Frank Aloise used candelabra to introduce Max Liebman spectacular.

Harvey Schmidt depicted hero's numerous wives in feature film.

Gangland motif was used by Georg Olden for Studio One melodrama.

8

Lavish use of color distinguished Hall of Fame title card by Harvey Schmidt.

Occupations of panel show's guests were gaily burlesqued by artist Roy Doty.

"Two years ago I bought my first Color TV—now I have 200 of them!"

says *Mr. Bertram Weal*, General Manager of New York's luxurious Hotel Tuscany on 39th St. near Park Ave.

"We pride ourselves on all the latest conveniences at the Tuscany," says Mr. Weal. "That now includes Color TV. And as a Color TV owner for two years, I predict enthusiastic approval from our guests. The picture is clear and natural. As for dependability . . . well, we had no hesitation in putting it in *every* room of the hotel. That should be recommendation for anyone."

RCA Victor Color TV has proved so dependable you can now buy it with a free 1-year warranty on all parts and tubes, including the picture tube.* See for yourself at any RCA Victor dealer's. Prices from $495.   *excluding labor

SANFORD,
smart consolette
in new Mark Series

At your service: RCA Victor Factory Service Contracts from $39.95 (90 days). Manufacturer's nationally advertised VHF list price shown. UHF optional, extra. Prices, specifications subject to change.

RCA VICTOR
RADIO CORPORATION OF AMERICA

RCA PIONEERED AND DEVELOPED COMPATIBLE COLOR TV

New SEVILLE 21 by RCA Victor. In mahogany or blond tropical hardwood finish, $795. Not shown: DIRECTOR 21, $895.

"It's Big Color that makes TV entertainment spectacular"

SAYS BOB HOPE soon to be seen in "That Certain Feeling"
—a Paramount Picture—

"I'm not kidding when I say Big Color TV is sensational. We've had our RCA Victor set eight months now. Delores and the kids love it. Me, I'm plain hypnotized.

"The World Series looked so real I almost tossed a pop bottle at the ump. Watching football, the players practically tumble into your lap. And a Big Color *musical* outdazzles even a California rainbow. I tell you, these RCA people know Color TV from the inside. And it shows on the outside."

Your RCA Victor dealer invites you to watch Big Color TV on the same set Bob Hope talks about. Afterwards, see a Black-and-White program in sharp, clear Black-and-White on the same set. (It's like having two sets in one.) Phone your dealer now.

WORRY-FREE! With an RCA Victor Factory Service Contract (optional, extra) you get expert installation and maintenance. Available in most areas, but only to RCA Victor TV owners. • Manufacturer's nationally advertised UHF-VHF prices shown, subject to change.

RCA VICTOR Tmks ® RADIO CORPORATION OF AMERICA

RCA pioneered and developed Compatible Color TV

The new Director 21. UHF-VHF tuner. Two extra-large speakers. Blond tropical hardwood finish. Also in mahogany finish (model 21CT662), **$895.**

BIG COLOR BY RCA VICTOR

The final touch of beauty in TV—ready for you now in your choice of two new 21-inch Color TV sets.

Your guests arrive. One of them notices your handsome new TV set. You turn it on, not saying a word. Then . . . "Oh, it's *Color* TV!" someone exclaims.

Listen to their excited comments. How big the picture is! (It's *big* 21-inch TV – in color.) How *true* the colors are! (This is the special meaning of Big Color by RCA Victor.)

Then you tell them about the won-ders you watch in brilliant color. Spec-taculars . . . stirring plays . . . college football. And because this is Com-patible Color, pioneered and developed by RCA, you see black-and-white pro-grams in black-and-white, too!

This is a picture that can come to life for you *now*. The first step: phone your RCA Victor dealer. He is holding an invitation for you — to see an actual colorcast on RCA Victor Color TV some evening soon!

Worry-Free! With an RCA Victor Factory Service Contract (optional, extra) you get expert installation and maintenance. Avail-able in most TV areas but only to RCA Victor TV owners.

See Milton Berle, Martha Raye on NBC-TV alternately, 2 out of every 3 Tuesdays. Don't miss NBC-TV's "Pro-ducers' Showcase" in RCA Compatible Color or black-and-white, NBC-TV, Nov. 14. KIDS! Enter Colgate's big "Name the Tugboat" contest. See "Howdy Doody" in Color on NBC-TV at your RCA Victor dealer's.

Manufacturer's nationally advertised UHF-VHF list prices shown, subject to change.

The new Seville 21. UHF-VHF tuner. Mahogany or blond tropical hardwood finish (21CT661), **$795.**

RCA VICTOR
Tmks ®   RADIO CORPORATION OF AMERICA   "HIS MASTER'S VOICE"

FIRST IN BLACK-AND-WHITE TELEVISION • FIRST IN COMPATIBLE COLOR TELEVISION

The face is familiar, but what color are his eyes ?

LOOK AND SEE................

All RCA Victor Big Color TV sets bring you a *full 250 square inches* of viewable picture. Shown: **Haviland 21** (21CT660). Mahogany or limed oak grained finishes. **$695.**

THE WONDER WORLD OF COLOR IS YOURS
WITH RCA VICTOR BIG COLOR TV FROM $695

And what a big, wide, colorful world it is! The picture you see here can't possibly show *all* that Big Color adds to TV—the realism, the depth, the emotion, the *impact*, the almost unbelievable beauty. For this is an entirely new kind of TV entertainment—Big Color TV by RCA Victor—yours at the lowest price in history.

Musicals, comedy, drama, children's shows—you see them all *clearly, sharply* on beautiful RCA Victor Big Color TV. And the colors are true-to-life, rich, stunning—incomparable!

Add Color to your family's TV life *now*. Stop in at your RCA Victor dealer's for a *free* demonstration of RCA Victor Big Color TV!

With an RCA Victor Factory Service Contract (optional, extra) your set is installed and serviced by RCA's own technicians. Available only to RCA Victor TV owners.

LIKE HAVING 2 SETS IN 1

You tune in both color programs and black-and-white shows on every RCA Victor Big Color TV set! This is Compatible Color, pioneered and developed by RCA.

See Milton Berle, Martha Raye alternately on NBC-TV, 2 out of every 3 Tuesdays. And see NBC-TV's spectacular "Producers' Showcase" in Color or Black-and-White, Monday, April 30. • Manufacturer's nationally advertised UHF-VHF prices shown, subject to change.

Director 21 (21CT662). Mahogany or blond tropical hardwood finishes. **$895.**

Gainsborough 21 (21CT664). 3 speakers. Natural walnut or maple finishes. **$995.**

RCA VICTOR
Tmks® RADIO CORPORATION OF AMERICA

FIRST IN BLACK-AND-WHITE TELEVISION • FIRST IN COMPATIBLE COLOR TELEVISION

M OST of his admirers have never seen more than a shadow of the real Maurice Chevalier.

It takes the vibrancy, the vitality, the glowing realism of full color to present Chevalier as he really is, with his blue eyes twinkling and the laughter of all Paris on his lips. And that is exactly how he will appear Sunday, May 20th, on another NBC Sunday Spectacular produced by Max Liebman.

Other great Sunday Spectaculars — part of NBC's heavy schedule of Big Color programs — are now in preparation. Each is a triumph of television showmanship when it is seen in black and white — an outright revelation in color. Don't miss Chevalier, May 20th on NBC Television. Don't miss *any* of the Sunday Spectaculars starring the most heralded entertainers in show business. And see them all live in color if you possibly can!

EXCITING THINGS ARE HAPPENING ON

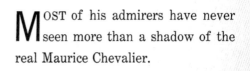

NBC Television

a service of

RCA

My second most prized possession

There is a great temptation to address George Preston Marshall as "Chief." That's because his most prized possession is the *Redskins*, Washington's professional football team—symbolized here by a professional wooden Indian.

Being a sportsman, Mr. Marshall thrives on action, excitement and spectacle. The same reasons why he picks RCA Victor Color TV as his second most prized possession. It's the most exciting way to enjoy television, and the only way to appreciate the many fine color programs. Without question, Color TV is the best television there is. That is why it keeps making a place for itself with more and more people like George Preston Marshall. People who lead the colorful life.

RCA Victor offers a wide selection of Color TV models. Some—like Mr. Marshall's *Grenoble* model, above—come equipped with remote control push-button tuning. Your dealer will be glad to arrange a demonstration for you. RCA Victor Color TV as low as $495.

ON THE 5TH ANNIVERSARY OF COLOR TV. SEE THE DIFFERENCE COLOR TV MAKES

Turn this page
to find out what
you're missing,
on the TV shows
you never miss!...

The second most prized possession of Rodgers and Hammerstein

You probably know all about them. You certainly don't need a long introduction to Rodgers and Hammerstein, the men who created a whole new musical theater.

A simple flower drum, symbolic of "Flower Drum Song," is their most prized possession. R&H's second most prized possession is today's RCA Victor Color TV.

For they have worked in color television. They believe in it, and know how exciting it is. The Rodgers and Hammerstein television production of "Cinderella" received rave reviews. Critic after critic singled out the colors of sets and costumes for special praise. R&H know that on television or on the stage,

color is a vital force in setting a mood—heightening the action—actually giving the audience more enjoyment.

Whether your taste runs to musicals or westerns, sports or comedy, RCA Victor "Living Color" TV is the way to watch any show. The color picture is brilliant, the black-and-white picture of finest quality, too. And the sound system is so advanced, it can serve as the second speaker unit for your Stereo High Fidelity setup. See RCA Victor Color TV at your dealer's. Prices as low as $495.

ON THE 5TH ANNIVERSARY OF COLOR TV, SEE THE DIFFERENCE COLOR TV MAKES

the big thrill of
BIG COLOR!

Why miss it another day? Whatever kind of program *you* like best, see it glowing and vibrant in a new light! Here's the wide and wonderful choice of Big Color TV shows on NBC . . . in the month of June *alone*.

Eighteen full-hour plays, live from Hollywood on MATINEE THEATER! A SUNDAY SPECTACULAR! MAX LIEBMAN PRESENTS *"Sweethearts"! A 90-minute production of "Happy Birthday" on* PRODUCERS' SHOWCASE! THE MILTON BERLE SHOW! *And that's not all! All these top-rated NBC programs are giving one or more Big Color performances during June, too!* KRAFT TELEVISION THEATER! GOODYEAR PLAYHOUSE! THIS IS YOUR LIFE! THE COMEDY HOUR! THE DINAH SHORE SHOW!

Yes, NBC is color-vising the kind of programs *you* like . . . right now! And by the end of summer, NBC will bring you at least one Big Color TV program *every evening!* You can, of course, enjoy them all in black and white. But discover NBC Big Color and you'll see how much you've been missing . . . on the shows you never miss.

NBC TELEVISION

exciting things are happening on ———●━ *a service of* ⓡⒸⒶ

Like 2 sets in 1! New easy-to-tune, depend

It's your smartest investment in TV today—actually costs only a few cents a day more than black-and-white alone! And you'll enjoy "Living Color" for years to come!

Now you can enjoy dazzling co shows *every single night of the week* on m NBC-TV stations. It's a billion-dollar wo of entertainment, yet RCA Victor brings to you in "Living Color" at a new low co You see pictures that are crisply defined vividly lifelike. You get this superb formance because dependable RCA Vic Big Color is *ready . . . right now!*

What's more, Big Color TV tunes i wink! Just two simple knobs control color that big 21-inch picture tube (overall di

S EASY AS FLIPPING THESE PAGES,

CA VICTOR COMPATIBLE BIG COLOR TV

WITCHES FROM CRISP BLACK-AND-WHITE

TO "LIVING COLOR"

Big Color TV by RCA Victor—from $495!

—with 254 sq. in. of viewable picture. because this is *Compatible* Color, you gular telecasts in black-and-white, too. ke 2 sets in 1!

the sound is fabulous! Four Big models have superb Balanced Fidelity d. All Deluxe models bring you magnif-*three* speaker Panoramic Sound!

see for yourself how wonderful Big is—how easily you can own it. Visit RCA Victor dealer's and choose *your*

set from ten spectacular new styles. Ask your dealer about easy budget terms. Better do it today. After all, it's nearly Christmas . . . and this one exciting gift could be the perfect answer to your family shopping problem.

Symbol of RCA Victor Compatible Color TV

RCA VICTOR
Tmks. ® RADIO CORPORATION OF AMERICA

RCA PIONEERED AND DEVELOPED COMPATIBLE COLOR TELEVISION

SONJA HENIE ICE REVUE, DEC. 22, ON NBC.
EXCITING THINGS ARE HAPPENING EVERY NIGHT ON

NBC COLOR TELEVISION

Like 2 sets in 1! New easy-to-tune, depend

It's your smartest investment in TV today—actually costs only a few cents a day more than black-and-white alone! And you'll enjoy "Living Color" for years to come!

Now you can enjoy dazzling co shows *every single night of the week* on r NBC-TV stations. It's a billion-dollar w of entertainment, yet RCA Victor bring to you in "Living Color" at a new low c You see pictures that are crisply define vividly lifelike. You get this superb formance because dependable RCA Vi Big Color is *ready . . . right now!*

What's more, Big Color TV tunes wink! Just two simple knobs control colo that big 21-inch picture tube (overall d

Big Color TV by RCA Victor—from $495!

—with 254 sq. in. of viewable picture. ... because this is *Compatible* Color, you ... egular telecasts in black-and-white, too. ...ike 2 sets in 1!

...n the sound is fabulous! Four Big ...r models have superb Balanced Fidelity ...d. All Deluxe models bring you magnif-...t *three* speaker Panoramic Sound!

...see for yourself how wonderful Big ...r is—how easily you can own it. Visit ... RCA Victor dealer's and choose *your*

set from ten spectacular new styles. Ask your dealer about easy budget terms. Better do it today. After all, it's nearly Christmas ... and this one exciting gift could be the perfect answer to your family shopping problem.

Symbol of RCA Victor Compatible Color TV

RCA VICTOR
Tmks. ® RADIO CORPORATION OF AMERICA

RCA PIONEERED AND DEVELOPED COMPATIBLE COLOR TELEVISION

107

Aldrich. Mahogany grained or limed oak grained finishes. Stand optional, extra. Model 21CS781. $495.

Whitby Deluxe. 3-speaker Panoramic Sound. Mahogany or blond tropical hardwood veneers and solids. Model 21CD789. $695.

Chandler Deluxe. 3-speaker Panoramic Sound. Mahogany or natural walnut veneers and solids. Model 21CD793. $795.

Like 2 sets in 1! New easy-to-tune, depend

It's your smartest investment in TV today—actually costs only a few cents a day more than black-and-white alone! And you'll enjoy "Living Color" for years to come!

Now you can enjoy dazzling co shows *every single night of the week* on n NBC-TV stations. It's a billion-dollar w of entertainment, yet RCA Victor bring to you in "Living Color" at a new low c You see pictures that are crisply define vividly lifelike. You get this superb formance because dependable RCA Vi Big Color is *ready . . . right now*!

What's more, Big Color TV tunes i wink! Just two simple knobs control colo that big 21-inch picture tube (overall di

Stanwyck. Mahogany grained
or limed oak grained finishes.
Model 21CT783. $550.

Westcott. Mahogany grained
or limed oak grained finishes.
Model 21CT785. $595.

Asbury Deluxe. "Color-Quick" tuning.
Mahogany, walnut or blond tropical
hardwood finishes. Model 21CD791. $750.

...mouth. Mahogany grained, walnut
...ed or limed oak grained finishes.
...el 21CT786. $650.

Arliss Deluxe. Chinese Chippendale
styling in mahogany veneers and solids.
Model 21CD797. $850.

Big Color TV by RCA Victor—from $495!

—with 254 sq. in. of viewable picture.
...because this is *Compatible* Color, you
...egular telecasts in black-and-white, too.
...ike 2 sets in 1!

...the sound is fabulous! Four Big
...models have superb Balanced Fidelity
...d. All Deluxe models bring you magnif-
...three speaker Panoramic Sound!

...see for yourself how wonderful Big
...r is—how easily you can own it. Visit
...RCA Victor dealer's and choose *your*

set from ten spectacular new styles. Ask
your dealer about easy budget terms. Better
do it today. After all, it's nearly Christmas . . .
and this one exciting gift could be the perfect answer to your family shopping problem.

AT YOUR SERVICE. RCA Victor Factory Service Contracts
covering installation and servicing are available in most TV
areas, from $39.95—but only to RCA Victor TV owners.

Manufacturer's nationally advertised VHF list prices shown.
UHF optional, extra. Some models slightly higher far West,
South, and Canada. Prices and specifications subject to change
without notice.

Symbol of RCA Victor Compatible Color TV

RCA VICTOR
Tmks. ® RADIO CORPORATION OF AMERICA

"HIS MASTER'S VOICE"

RCA PIONEERED AND DEVELOPED COMPATIBLE COLOR TELEVISION

The REGENT 21* Fabulous Color TV in rich, mahogany grained cabinet with graceful tapered legs. 255 sq. in. aluminized Color-Magic picture tube. Powerful new Color TV Chassis. Inclined, easy-to-read tuning dial. Wide range FM sound system with heavy duty 8″ PM speaker. Also in modern blonde oak grained finish.

he PRESIDENT 21* Imposing Color TV Con-
e with blonde oak grained finish. Has 255 sq. in.
minized Color-Magic picture tube. "Royal 600" Chas-
Lighted, inclined dial. Twin PM speakers with "staged range" response for extended bass, greater sound
tput. Also in traditional mahogany grained finish.

The PATRICIAN 21* Luxurious Color TV with
high fidelity sound! Stunning genuine Sierra veneers.
Beautiful superbly crafted credenza cabinet. Has 255 sq.
in. aluminized Color-Magic tube. Lighted, inclined dial.
New "Royal 600" Chassis. Also in genuine blonde oak
or mahogany wood veneers.

*Overall diagonal.

GENUINE HIGH
FIDELITY SOUND

4 matched speakers and
amplifier fill your room
with rich, full-range sound!

CONVENIENT TOP
FRONT TUNING

Admiral tuning dials are on
top, up front where they
belong. Tune standing up.

(A) **Aldrich.** Mahogany-, limed oak-grained finishes. (21CS781.) $495. Stand, opt., extra. (B) **Stanwyck.** Limed oak-, mahogany-grained finishes. (21CT783.) $550. (C) **Westcott.** Mahogany-, limed-oak grained fir (21CT785.) $595. (D) **Dartmouth.** Walnut-, mahogany-, limed oak-grained finishes. (21CT786.) $650. Deluxe models: (E) **Whitby.** Blond tropical hdwd., mah. veneers and solids. (21CD789.) $695. (F) **Asbury.** N

COLOR EVERY NIGHT! See it on new

Spectacular increase in Color shows! NBC-TV alone is scheduling Color for *every night in the week—starting this Fall*. Make this *your* year for Big Color TV!

SYMBOL OF RCA VICTOR COMPATIBLE COLOR TV

RCA VICTOR SALUTES NATIONAL TELEVISION WEEK SEPT. 23-29
Celebrating the finest home entertainment in sight

Spectacular news! Starting this Fall, there'll be an exciting TV s or Spectacular in Color over NBC-TV every single night! V wonderful news—since right now you can walk into your I Victor's dealer's and buy new Big Color TV for as little as $495!

This is the ultimate in television. Cabinetry that rivals fine fu ture—performance and dependability that measure up to I Victor's highest standards—and a BIG 21-inch tube (overall di eter), with a full 254 square inches of viewable picture. And v a picture it is!

Spectacular "Living Color" picture. Every one of the 10 new Color sets presents a masterpiece picture in brilliant "Living Co —the most natural tones you've ever seen. And all six *Deluxe*

, mah., blond trop. hdwd. finishes. (21CD791.) $750. **(G) Strathmore.** French walnut, bleached birch veneers and solids. (21CD795.) $795. **(H) Chandler.** Nat. walnut, mah. veneers and solids. (21CD793.) $795. iss. Mah. veneers and solids. (21CD797.) $850. **(J) Wingate.** Maple, French walnut veneers and solids. (21CD799.) $850. **Each Big Color set has 21-inch tube (overall diameter), 254 sq. in. viewable picture.**

CA Victor Big Color TV—as low as $495

ure RCA Victor automatic Chroma Control, equalizing color nsity from station to station, for *full fidelity* performance!

ctacular sound! Four Big Color models provide famous Balanced lity Sound. And the six new Deluxe models feature new 3-speaker oramic Sound that adds a new dimension to TV enjoyment.

ctacular "Color-Quick" tuning! In VHF and UHF too. Adjust the Color knobs, and the picture pops onto the screen. That's all e is to it—a child can do it! So visit your RCA Victor dealer's week. Ask for a free demonstration of RCA Victor *double-value* —at his store, or in your own home. Easy payment plan arranged.

acturer's nationally advertised list prices shown. UHF optional, extra. Slightly higher for West and South. cations and prices subject to change. Models available in Canada. Special 90-day Big Color RCA Victor y Service Contract available in most areas, only $39.95.

LIKE HAVING 2 SETS IN 1.
RCA Victor Big Color TV brings you both black-and-white and Color programs because it's *compatible!*

RCA VICTOR

Tmks.® RADIO CORPORATION OF AMERICA

RCA PIONEERED AND DEVELOPED COMPATIBLE COLOR TELEVISION

before your

Television has become Color Television . . . *before your very eyes!*

And it's Big Color! Producers' Showcase, The Sunday Spectaculars, Max Liebman Presents, Maurice Evans' Hallmark Hall of Fame—each a lavish, ninety-minute production in which the brightest stars of the entertainment world are proud to appear. The NBC Opera Theatre, presenting the world's greatest operas in skillful English translations. NBC Matinee Theater, the hour-long dramatic show that has set new standards for daytime television. Milton Berle, who made Tuesday night a national laugh night. The American premiere of Laurence Olivier's great motion picture, "Richard III." Howdy Doody,

always the merriest and best loved of all the children's progra

Then there are special features like "Antarctica" and "Assignm India," and special events, like the World Series and the Rose B Parade. Color telecasts of shows usually seen in black-and-white, the Dinah Shore Show, the George Gobel Show, the Jimmy Dura Show, and Zoo Parade.

And more to come . . . and then more again!

By the end of the summer, another $12,000,000 in new color stu and facilities will bring you more shows and bigger shows in Co

very eyes!

...nd wait till you see them exactly as they are planned and produced—
...with the bright costumes, the vivid sets, the actors and actresses in
...ll their glowing vitality!

...t's all happening right now, on NBC. Hard to believe? Sit down
...efore a Color TV set and *see* it happening—*before your very eyes.*

...xciting things are happening on

NBC TELEVISION (RCA)
a service of

...and through

the Wonderland

The storybook Alice toured Wonderland alone. But now ther
new Wonderland that the whole family can visit . . . through
"looking glass" of a color television set.

Already this year, NBC Big Color has filled this fabulous loo
glass with wonder upon wonder. Great plays like "The Bar
of Wimpole Street" and "The Taming of the Shrew." Memor

this looking glass...

f NBC Big Color TV!

certs like "Festival of Music" and "The Music of Gershwin."
zling Spectaculars like "Marco Polo" and "Paris in the Spring-
e." And many of NBC's brightest stars—like Arlene Francis,
n Martin and Jerry Lewis, Ralph Edwards, Maurice Evans,
ah Shore, Eddie Fisher, Tennessee Ernie Ford.

inning early this Fall, NBC plans to present at least one major

Big Color television show *every evening!* Has *your* Alice seen this
new Wonderland of color television? She'll love it. And so will you!

exciting things
are happening
in color on **NBC** television *a service of* **RCA**

LEFT: A supermarket seemed like an unlikely place to see color television in the mid-1950s, but not to one RCA east coast distributor, who placed sets in local supermarkets to catch the eye of busy housewives who were out grocery shopping. To rope in the kiddies, RCA and Birdseye co-sponsored a coloring contest that would make a hundred winning young entrants proud owners of RCA color sets. ABOVE AND BELOW: Typical interior and exterior of mid-1960s to 1970s "mom and pop" color television dealers. The sets were huge, the dealers small. The beautiful wood cabinet consoles not only took up a lot of floor space, but since independent dealers were also out-of-pocket the cost to purchase sets for their showroom models, the number of color television sets a dealer displayed were limited. That's where sales catalogs came into play, allowing dealers to show off every model of a television set in beautifully rendered illustrations or photographs to a potential customer. Not until the advent of super-sized electronic retailers like Good Guys, Best Buy, and Circuit City were television sets displayed in great numbers on showroom floors, allowing dealers to dispense with lushly illustrated catalogs created to expedite sales.

MAGIC?

IT'S THE MAGIC OF COLOR TV AND YOU CAN SEE IT EVERY DAY!

Yes, you *can* believe your eyes! There's a steady stream of Color on NBC every night and every day. And what a difference NBC Color makes! See it on big NBC special shows like the 90-minute Festival of Magic (May 27) and The Jerry Lewis Show (June 8). And enjoy it on dozens of your favorite *regularly-scheduled* NBC programs, too!

NBC Color adds to the drama of Robert Montgomery Presents, Kraft Television Theatre, Lux Video Theatre, Alcoa-Goodyear Playhouse, and Matinee Theatre. NBC Color brightens up Dinah Shore's Chevy Show, The Life of Riley, Ray Bolger's Washington Square, and Adventures of Sir Lancelot. And programs like the new Eddie Fisher-George Gobel Show, the new Dean Martin Show, The Steve Allen Show, and Jack Barry's "21" will all be coming to you in NBC Color, too!

Make this Monday's Festival of Magic the first show you see on your new Color TV set. There'll be more magic on that set, night after night, day after day. All you have to do is tune in NBC.

NBC COLOR TELEVISION

The CHALFONT, one of three
popular lowboy designs.

You don't know what you're missing 'til you get new RCA VICTOR COLOR TV!

The Wireless Wizard, only remote control with *master-off*, changes programs, adjusts volume and color—turns the set *completely* off!

New Vista tuner, heart of the set, is the most sensitive ever designed. It gives you clearer pictures from hard-to-get stations!

Year warranty on all parts, including the picture tube. 5-year warranty on Security Sealed circuit boards. Labor costs excluded.

You just don't know how exciting television can be 'til you see RCA Victor Color TV.

You'll see pictures in sharp, clear color, beautifully true to life. You'll see the big, talked-about TV programs at their finest. You'll get clear, detailed black and white on the same set, too. Controls are easy to operate, and the set is dependable—*RCA* dependable!

The new models are many and handsome—and priced for *you*. See them at your RCA Victor dealer's today. There's no TV like Color TV.

Service is no problem. See your local dealer, serviceman, or nearest RCA Service Co. Specifications subject to change without notice. UHF, optional, extra.

TMK(s) ®

The Most Trusted Name in Television

RADIO CORPORATION OF AMERICA

On November 4—see listing in this issue for time and channel

"Another Evening with Fred Astaire"—
See the difference Color TV makes

Capture all the imagination, the artistry, the personality of Fred Astaire. See him true-to-life in color. The mood, the atmosphere, the twinkling changes—all that makes up show business: COLOR. See the difference color makes. RCA Victor Color TV prices start at just $495. Worth it? See it in color and you won't settle for anything less.

THE ATHERTON

RCA VICTOR
RADIO CORPORATION OF AMERICA

RCA Victor – for color so rea

New Hi-Lite Color Tube with Perma-Chrome.

Something special has been added to RCA Victor's new big-screen color TV. It's RCA's new rectangular Hi-Lite Tube with Perma-Chrome. And the way it works is beautiful to behold. Ordinary rectangular tubes can produce distorted colors while they're warming up. The Hi-Li Tube with Perma-Chrome delivers uniform color purity the moment the picture comes on. An it keeps it there for as long as you keep on viewing. What else do you get in RCA Victor Mark II

you'll think you are there!

See Walt Disney's "Wonderful World of Color," Sundays, NBC-TV Network. Shown above, The Abbey.

...olor TV? A super-sensitive New Vista® VHF Tuner linked to a 25,000 volt ...hassis for big picture-pulling power. And a solid integrated circuit ...the sound system for exceptional reliability. See your RCA Victor dealer ...or a demonstration. You can't miss his store. It's the most colorful place ...town. RCA Victor—The color TV pioneer.

Tmk(s)*

The Most Trusted Name in Electronics

RCA VICTOR PRESENTS COLOR TV WIT

Brings you color so bright, so tr

Now comes a glorious, lifelike color picture up to 50% brighter . . . plus New Vista picture-pulling power . . . plus a wide and wonderful choice of new models . . . plus dependability you can count on!

You've never seen TV like this before! RCA' High-Fidelity Color tube brings you a bea color picture that is up to 50% brighter . . . a vastl proved black-and-white picture . . . the tremendous p power of RCA Victor's revolutionary New Vista tune glare-proof picture tube on many models cuts distra reflections . . . simplified controls, easier tuning . . . bu dependability in every circuit and tube from RCA—

See Walt Disney's new "Wonderful World of Color" series, starting Sunday, over NBC-TV Network.

EW HIGH-FIDELITY PICTURE TUBE!

you have to see it to believe it!

er in developing and perfecting Color television. Look
ne programming: sports events . . . color dramas . . .
icals . . . spectaculars—an average of almost 40 hours
twork color every week! Plus *local* color programs! See
RCA Victor dealer for a demonstration of new Color
You have to see it to believe it! Prices start as low as $495.

e is no problem. See your local dealer, serviceman, or nearest RCA Service
ationally advertised list price shown, optional with dealer. Slightly higher
South. UHF, optional, extra. Price, specifications subject to change. Tmk(s)®

Your RCA Victor Color Television
is a rugged instrument, built by the
pioneer in perfecting Color TV.

The Most Trusted Name in Color Television

RADIO CORPORATION OF AMERICA

From the World Leader in Color TV
...UNSURPASSED NATURAL COLOR

MARK 8

MARK 8

New "MARK 8" COLOR TV by RCA VICTOR

See RCA Victor's Unsurpassed Color
Picture...from the RCA proved-in-use
High-Fidelity Color Tube...a Picture up
to 50% brighter than with any Previous
Color Tube...Color so bright...so clear
...you have to see it to believe it!

RCA pioneered color television. RCA started resea
ing it 20 years before RCA Victor introduced c
television sets publicly in 1954.

And today's new "Mark 8" Color TV by RCA Vi
climaxes 8 years of actual performance in American home

RCA Victor made color TV a reality...made it depend
...proved it in homes like yours from coast to coast for e
years. These are all reasons why more people own RCA Vi
Color Television than any other kind.

Two major networks have booked many of your favo
shows in color ... Hazel, Bonanza, Laramie, World Se
Football, Walt Disney's "Wonderful World of Color"
many new shows ... plus programs from leading local stati
In many localities, this will average as much as 7 hours a

MARK 8   MARK 8

Pictured from left to right are the Bentley, Burgoyne, Abbeville and Gaynor.

limaxing 8 years <u>home</u> proved performance!

what's behind RCA Victor "Mark 8" Color TV that puts it ahead

Picture" RCA High-Fidelity Color Tube proved in use to give a picture up to 50% iter than any previous color tube. Delivers lly fine pictures in black-and-white. All ole and consolette models feature glare- f safety glass for better viewing.

Vista Chassis, super powered and equipped RCA Victor's famed "New Vista" tuner— get unsurpassed picture-pulling power even any difficult TV signal areas. It is the most nced TV chassis ever built by RCA Victor.

Modern Security Sealed Circuits, RCA Security Sealed Circuits use precision-crafted, copper-etched and permanently bonded circuit boards to eliminate more than 200 hand-wired, hand-soldered connections found in old-fashioned circuitry. This modern way is your assurance of more dependable performance.

"Wireless Wizard" full-function remote control, available on many models, changes channels, adjusts volume up or down, controls color and tint, and turns the set completely off!

"Big Picture" Color TV for as little as $495 (for the Fraser, not shown). Manufacturer's nationally advertised price, optional with dealer. Slightly higher some areas West, South. UHF optional extra. Prices, specifications subject to change.

See Walt Disney's "Wonderful World of Color" Sundays, NBC-TV Network.

RCA **The Most Trusted Name in Television**

Tmk(s)®

129

Now color TV doesn't have to be big to be good.

Take a look.

We've put every bit of our color console know-how into Porta-Color.

Unlike the big boys, Porta-Color can be carried around, from room to room, with one hand.

And it's half the price. $269.95.*

Of course, if you like big screen color that also happens to be a beautiful piece of furniture, tune in our color consoles with "Meter Guide" tuning.

It's a General Electric exclusive. It takes

all the guesswork out of getting a good color picture.

In portable size or console size, G.E. gives you juicy color.

Still not sold?

Take another look.

GENERAL ELECTRIC

RCA invites 2,000 people with $2,000 to leap into the year 2000.

Most changes are made gradually. A little here. A little there. But in one giant step, we've unveiled a new century in color television.

Introducing the RCA set of the future: The Two Thousand.

It's a limited edition (2000 sets, $2000* each) with unlimited advancement.

First and most obvious, is its 21st-century design. Sitting like a silent spaceship, its sculptured whiteness curves to a rosewood veneer top. The black translucent doors slide back and disappear into the set, revealing the 23-inch diagonal screen.

And what a picture you'll see on that screen.

It's our new Hi-Lite 70 tube—computer-designed and engineered for 100% more brightness than any big screen color tube we've ever made. The Hi-Lite 70 tube gives such a vivid, detailed picture, you can

The Two Thousand

even watch it in a brightly lit room.

The remote controls of color, tint and volume have electronic memories. They operate electronically. So there are no motors, no noise, and no moving parts to wear out or break down.

Inside the Two Thousand, though, is the biggest news.

We've eliminated the conventional VHF tuner. In its place are new computer-like "memory" circuits—electronic circuits with memories like tiny computers.

When you press the remote-control button, the circuits automatically remember which channels were active. So there's no wandering through empty VHF channels for the station you want. You simply go silently and instantly from one live station to the next.

It's all done electronically with solid state devices. Which means cool, dependable operation. And again, no motors, no noise, and no moving parts on VHF (one quiet motor on UHF)

The Two Thousand was made possible this soon with the help of computers. We used their speed and accuracy in many ways. To help design key systems. Or inspect them. Or test them for optimum performance and reliability.

Imagine. Once for $2000, all you got was a trip around the world. Now you can travel to a whole new century.

Computer Crafted Color

RCA

*$2000 price optional with dealer

5

TELEVISION BALLYHOO –
The Medium on a Fishhook

TELEVISION BALLYHOO –
The Medium on a Fishhook

In the decade after World War II, advertising agencies flush with marketing all kinds of consumer products wanted to tap into the public's newfound fascination with television. This connection could be as subtle as rendering a television set in the background of an ad, or it might be as prominent as linking Max Factor makeup to color television. RCA partnered with several consumer companies (in exchange for NBC airtime) in an extraordinary campaign to mutually promote their color-dependent products in print ads. For example, a series of Arrow Shirt ads displayed men's brightly colored shirts next to RCA color television sets.

Sometimes, though, a product's relationship to television was tenuous. It might even be bizarre. In one such case, artist Tom Hall illustrated a woman standing next to a television set trying to distract a man from watching a baseball game—for Kotex feminine hygiene pads. Perhaps the most disturbing connection to television—even if it was enlightening as far as how women were often represented in the 1950s—was an ad for Hotpoint dishwashers. In it, a housewife is stranded behind a wall of stacked dirty dishes while her husband and children, oblivious to her plight, enjoy a TV western on the other side of the porcelain barrier. Even the Indian on the television screen seems more aware of her dilemma—he looks absolutely appalled by how the woman is being treated by her family.

Renderings of women could also be whimsical. Artists Dick Sargent and Dink Siegel, who worked for General Food's ad agency, excelled at embodying the yin-and-yang extreme moods of teenage girls, with television sets as enablers in two ads. In the one Siegel illustrated for Jell-O in 1952, a young woman is vigorously exercising with a counterpart on her television screen, and in the other that Sargent executed in 1958, a girl is fast asleep in a chair next to her set after having consumed Post Toasties cereal. In the Jell-O ad, the television set acts as an "upper," inducing a manic high in the girl and causing her to work up a sweat. In the Toasties ad, the set (and possibly also the cereal) act as a muscle relaxer, allowing her to calm down and fall asleep.

The most interesting television-linked ad, albeit not the flashiest, has to be one with film actor Don Ameche. In 1939, Ameche was so convincing in his portrayal of Alexander Graham Bell in a big-screen biography that afterward many people believed that it was he, not Bell, who invented the telephone. The ad agency for Personna razor blades used this misimpression to cleverly connect Ameche's "inventive skill" to television in its 1947 ad. "Now I've got to invent television!" the headline states. "When I invented the telephone, I fixed it so you couldn't see through it. I didn't want anybody to spot my beard. But now that I use Personna Blades, I'm working day and night to perfect television. I want everybody to see the new, the well-groomed, *Personna*-fied Ameche. . . ."

And if Don Ameche had invented television, they would have.

Two ridiculous gimmicks of the 1940's.

Everyone laughed when they came out with the television.

A box that could show pictures from 3,000 miles away? Absurd.

But everyone really cracked up when we came out with the Volkswagen.

A car with its engine in the back? Its trunk in the front? And its radiator in neither the front nor the back?

It even looked like a joke.

But time marched on.

The television clicked.

The Volkswagen accelerated.

People liked the idea of a car that didn't drink gas like water. Or oil like water. Or, for that matter, didn't even drink water.

Some strange people even liked the idea that it was strange looking.

In fact, Detroit car makers now like the idea of the VW so much that they have decided to make their own.

But even with all those new small cars around, the fate of the bug is still secure.

This is the first year for all of the others.

We've had twenty-three years of re-runs.

STARRING IN MILLIONS OF HOMES!

"fresh up" with Seven-Up!

BE A "FRESH UP" FAMILY!

Mom and Dad enjoy the programs as much as their youngsters do. And naturally, *all-family* fun means chilled bottles of 7-Up—the *all-family* drink. Sparkling 7-Up with its fresh, clean taste and delicate flavor, appeals to all ages . . . children and grownups alike. Cheerful 7-Up is so pure . . . so good . . . so wholesome they all can enjoy that "fresh up" family feeling.

Let the happy *all-family* drink add to your *all-family* fun often. Keep tempting, lively 7-Up in your refrigerator always. Buy a case wherever you see those bright 7-Up signs on display.

You like it ··· it likes you!

"Fresh Up" with 7up IT LIKES YOU

BUY A CASE TODAY!

Turn a Snack into a SUPER TREAT

See "SUPER CIRCUS" on Television starring beautiful MARY HARTLINE

WITH AMERICA'S

Ginger-Upper!

the finest ginger ale you've ever tasted!

For a deliciously *different* soda—put your favorite flavor ice cream in a tall glass and fill with Canada Dry Ginger Ale. It's a new taste thrill!

Dig into a dish of delicious cookies. Tasty? Right...and they taste even more wonderful than ever with Canada Dry Ginger Ale.

What better way to enjoy crispy pretzels than to top them off with a cool glass of sparkling Canada Dry Ginger Ale!

Like fresh, crisp potato chips? You don't know how really good they can taste... till you try them with refreshing Canada Dry Ginger Ale!

Treat yourself, your family and friends like visiting royalty. Turn a refrigerator raid into a rare banquet. Just load a tray with a couple of cool bottles of Canada Dry Ginger Ale and some tall glasses. Surround with plenty of snacks. Then pitch in and enjoy yourselves!

Seems as if just about *everything* tastes better with America's "Ginger-Upper!" It's got that exciting flavor of purest Jamaica ginger. It's got the dryness that never tires your taste. And it's as wholesome as any food you can serve. How many bottles of Canada Dry Ginger Ale in your refrigerator right now? Better stock up.

CANADA DRY

6 INDIVIDUAL BOTTLES

Get the Pick-Up Pak, 6 individual-sized bottles

CANADA DRY GINGER ALE · CANADA DRY WATER · CANADA DRY Spur COLA · Hi-Spot · CANADA DRY ORANGE SODA · CANADA DRY ROOT BEER

look for these labels... make friends of your feet for life

Red Goose

RED GOOSE SHOES

Grace Walker SHOES

THE John C. Roberts Shoe

FOR PARTICULAR MEN

Members of a distinguished family

TOM CORBETT
SPACE CADET

Made by the *world's largest shoemakers*, it's natural
that these distinguished brands offer the utmost in comfort,
style, fine leather and long wear . . . shoes to fit every foot
and every footwear need. Look for these famous brands in the
yellow pages of your 'phone book. And tune in Saturday mornings
to Tom Corbett, Space Cadet on the Dumont TV network
—a favorite program with boys and girls—parents, too.

Styled and Built by *Friedman - Shelby* Division • International Shoe Company • Saint Louis • World's Largest Shoemakers

Fashion Televues of Spring

See them . . . love them . . . the beautiful Gold (Red) Cross
Shoes you'll find so much "in the picture," this spring.
New as tomorrow's telecast. And such scene-stealers—
with their gentle elegance and proud,
gracious lines. Each is a Fit-Tested fashion,
which means it keeps your step as young
as Springtime, itself.

A

B

D

C

Now, more than ever—
America's unchallenged shoe value

$8⁹⁵ · $10⁹⁵

Slightly higher in Canada

THESE STYLES $10.95. A. The Parfait.
B. The Melody. C. The Coquette.
D. The Chateau. On model's feet, The Swank.
On television screen, The Carnival $8.95.

GOLD RED CROSS SHOES

The United States Shoe Corporation, Cincinnati 7, Ohio. Gold Cross Shoes are manufactured and distributed in England by Somervell Bros., Ltd., in Australia by "Gold Cross Shoes,"
(Aust.) Pty. Ltd., in South Africa by Eddels (S. A.), Ltd., in New Zealand by Duckworth, Turner and Co., Ltd. Gold Cross Shoes are now being featured in Canada by leading retailers.

ut of color TV research comes

DRESSES BY CEIL C

WITH THIS NEW COLOR DISCOVERY YOU'LL LOOK EXQUISIT
T NEVER "MADE UP"...EVEN UNDER THE MOST GLARING LIGH

y Max Factor brings you a new concept in make-up,
covery that makes possible new subtle colors that
you a look of radiant natural beauty all other make-
ave strived for without success. He calls this great
make-up Hi-Fi.

Fi does for skin color tones what high fidelity does
ound. Hi-Fi achieves delicate gradations of color
before possible. It makes your natural skin tone
vibrantly alive.

u'll love the look of it . . . true natural beauty . . .

You'll like the feel of it . . . its new lighter texture, the
way it smooths on . . . the way it softens your skin.

This new idea in color for make-up was developed
to fill an urgent need created by color television. Exist-
ing colors in make-ups appeared harsh, unflattering,
unnatural. So the great TV studios called in Max Factor
because of his tremendous experience in color research
for make-up.

And Max Factor created for their exclusive use, the
new concept in make-up colors that was needed . . a

that stay smooth and radiant under the most glaring lig

Now—he translates this amazing high fidelity co
principle into a new fluid make-up *made for you*. Hi-
Today *you* can walk into a store and select your c
shade in Hi-Fi Fluid Make-up. The only make-up t
makes you look as if you had the most wonderful natu
color . . . with never a "made up" look! Six hig
flattering high fidelity skin tones.

Hi-Fi Fluid Make-Up by Max Factor **$1.75** plus tax

reat new make-up **hi-fi**

AX FACTOR'S FLUID MAKE-UP

IN NEW HIGH FIDELITY SKIN TONES NEVER POSSIBLE BEFOI

GOING
ON SALE
TO
THE PUBLIC
FOR
THE FIRST
TIME

MAX FACTOR
hi-fi
HIGH FIDELITY
FLUID MAKE-UP

Telecasting Tomorrow — Today!

T HIS modern miss looks at motoring in an ultramodern way • So she's keenly interested, of course, in the brilliant new Body by Fisher. It brings so much of tomorrow's comfort, luxury and smartness to the General Motors cars of today • And no wonder. It is actually the longest, widest, strongest Unisteel Body ever born of Fisher craftsmanship • It gives you greater room in which to take road-life easy. It treats you to seats that are rich in the comforts of fine living room furniture. It puts a sturdier, higher-crowned Turret Top overhead and more rigid, shockproof reenforcements all around — to add to your security • Then, for the best of good measure, it provides the fourfold advantages of Planned Vision — a wider windshield, a larger back window, a more conveniently positioned rearview mirror, and freedom from eyestrain by the use of genuine Safety *Plate* Glass in all glass areas • Here, certainly, are abundant reasons why you hear so many motorists now saying, "The buyword for '40 is Body by Fisher"—which means a General Motors car, of course.

• • •

"DRIVE A LA SALLE" is a mighty smart suggestion these days. And one thing that certainly makes it so is this top-flight car's new Unisteel Turret Top Body by Fisher. For instance, it provides the La Salle Special Sedan, "televised" above, with the new, stronger Hi-Test Safety Plate Glass in all door windows and Ventipanes as well as the windshield — a front seat that's much wider — a larger windshield — an 18% larger back window.

EASY ON THE EYES

Genuine Safety *Plate* Glass actually eliminates the distortion waves produced by ordinary safety "window" glass. What's more, exhaustive tests show that it reduces eyestrain 62% — and Body by Fisher provides this better visibility for all passengers, through all glass areas, in all of the new General Motors cars.

UNISTEEL TURRET TOP

BODY BY Fisher

GM GENERAL MOTORS

ON GENERAL MOTORS CARS ONLY:

ONTIAC • OLDSMOBILE • BUICK • LA SALLE • CADILLAC

144

Very personally yours

New luxury comes into your life—the day you discover the new Kotex. For it gives you the softness that fulfills your fondest dream of comfort. Actually . . .

Miracle softness that you've never known before! You see, *this* softness really lasts, holds its shape without sacrificing safety, because the new Kotex is made to stay soft while you wear it. Moreover . . .

You'll never have a moment's qualm, with those flat pressed ends that prevent revealing outlines. And with that exclusive safety center —designed for your extra protection.

Welcome features all . . . and all 3 absorbencies of Kotex provide them. You have a choice of Regular, Junior, Super, to answer your needs exactly. To help you maintain that carefree assurance . . . so very *personally* yours.

*more women choose Kotex** *than all other sanitary napkins*

Gun shoots electrons to "paint" a picture

RCA VICTOR concentrates on mass production of complex electronic instruments—using Shell Industrial Lubricants in many vital operations. Every year, more people buy RCA Victor than any other television.

UNSEEN, inside your TV set is a remarkable gun. Its job: to bombard the picture screen with billions of electrons—under perfect control—and thus create the moving images you watch as a television program.

The electron gun is typical of RCA Victor operations, for this company specializes in mass production of sensitive electronic instruments and their components. And since RCA must work with small tolerances, careful maintenance of its manufacturing equipment is stressed.

Major emphasis is placed on proper lubrication of RCA Victor production machines. Shell oils and greases are applied according to strict schedules which have been simplified by continually reducing the number of types of lubricants required. Today, RCA Victor is able to service its machines with many fewer lubricants, and—to quote its engineers—"with complete satisfaction."

Development of more versatile industrial lubricants is another example of Shell leadership in the petroleum industry. Shell Research results in better quality—more for your money—when you buy products bearing the Shell name and trade-mark.

146

Top Performer!

Fire-Chief gasoline performance adds new thrills in all your driving . . .

new fleetness in get-aways, new instant pick-up in traffic and new surging

smoothness on the hills. And best of all Fire-Chief is a *regular* price gasoline.

So fill up with top performing Fire-Chief today at your Texaco Dealer.

He's the best friend your car ever had.

. . . and don't forget the best motor oil your money can buy.

THE TEXAS COMPANY
TEXACO DEALERS IN ALL 48 STATES
Texaco Products are also distributed in Canada and Latin America

TUNE IN: On television — the **TEXACO STAR THEATER** starring **MILTON BERLE** — every Tuesday night.
On radio — Metropolitan Opera Broadcasts — every Saturday afternoon. See newspaper for time and station.

Now's the time for JELL-O

JELL-O
BRAND
GELATIN DESSERT
SIX DELICIOUS FLAVORS

While you're bending down, bend an ear! Grand-tasting, swell-eating Jell-O gelatin is one of the lowest-calorie popular desserts you can eat. Whether you're watching your weight or not, Jell-O sure makes swell eating!

Any corn flakes are real gone...
as long as they're Post Toasties

REAL GONE—THAT'S FOR SURE...both the miss and her corn flakes! They're Post Toasties—rolled and toasted a special way that keeps the sweet corn flavor in each curly bit o' crispness. No wonder folks call them the "little bit better" corn flakes. Go ahead—taste 'em yourself!

"ALL POST CEREALS HAPPEN TO BE JUST A LITTLE BIT BETTER"

Post

The Breakfast Foods of General Foods

Please... let your wife

Doing dishes the Hotpoint workless way is easy and costs only a few pennies a day. You simply put the dishes in the Hotpoint Automatic Dishwasher, turn one switch and the job's done. Everything—dishes, silverware, pots, pans and casseroles —is double-washed, double-rinsed and dried electrically.

OOK TO HOTPOINT FOR THE FINEST—FIRST!

RANGES • REFRIGERATO

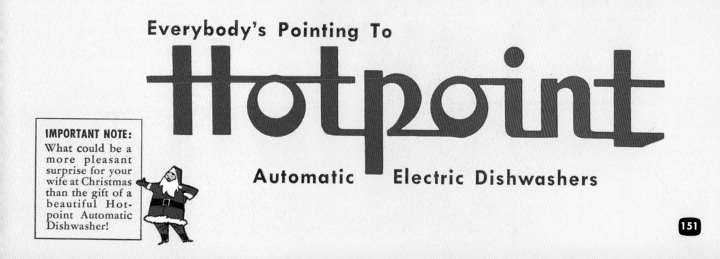

come into the living room

DON'T let dirty dishes make your wife a kitchen exile! She loses the most precious hours of her life shut off from pleasures of the family circle by the never-ending chore of old-fashioned dishwashing! Please . . . let her come into the living room. It's easy to banish the barrier of dishpan drudgery so she can join the family fun—the modern, automatic Hotpoint way!

● **The wonderful,** new Hotpoint Automatic Electric Dish-

washer is the greatest time- and labor-saving appliance ev[er] invented for the home. It also protects your family's health [by] doing dishes the sanitary way—many, many times cleaner th[an] is possible by hand. And it saves your wife at least an extra ho[ur] every day—seven hours a week—that she can devote to happ[y] home-making for the entire family! Hotpoint Inc. (*A Gene[ral] Electric Affiliate*), 5600 West Taylor Street, Chicago 44, Illino[is]

Everybody's Pointing To
Hotpoint

IMPORTANT NOTE: What could be a more pleasant surprise for your wife at Christmas than the gift of a beautiful Hotpoint Automatic Dishwasher!

Automatic   Electric   Dishwashers

[DISH]WASHERS • DISPOSALLS® • WATER HEATERS • FOOD FREEZERS • AUTOMATIC WASHERS • CLOTHES DRYERS • ROTARY IRONERS •

6

TELEVISION INTOXICANT

TELEVISION INTOXICANT

The consumer product ads most linked to television were those for liquor. From the beginning of television's post-war introduction, liquor ads (most prominently for beer and whiskey) featured television sets more prominently than they ever did radios. Why? Perhaps the biggest reason had to do with sporting events, which have always been popular occasions for drinking by spectators. With television, now fans could experience not only all the sounds, but also all the *sights* of big stadium contests, in the comfort of their living rooms. Then as now, television sports parties required the proper beverages. The most famous and longest-running beer/television print ads were part of a series sponsored by the United States Brewers Foundation (USBF).

The USBF series, entitled *Home Life in America,* ran from the 1940s through the late 1950s. The ads featuring television sets showed people drinking and socializing at home, usually watching a sporting event; they were illustrated by such renowned artists as Douglas Crockwell, Glenn Grohe, Pruett Carter, and John Falter. Television set manufacturer Admiral took notice of all the liquor consumption that took place during television viewing in many homes and decided to market to consumers in a more direct way. *Voila!* The Admiral Tele-bar was born in 1951 (see page 41), combining a television set, radio, phonograph, *and* bar—everything but the ice cubes. Because of its unique character, few Tele-bars were sold, making them a rare, highly prized collector's item.

Cocktails and a little telly, anyone?

FOR PLEASANT MOMENTS—"Look, Patrick, we're in television!
PM the Perfect Mixer gives another great performance . . .
a moving picture of Particular Mildness and taste in technicolor!"
"Aye, Michael, that's a mellow vision . . . and now let's hurry along . . .
people will be calling for a personal appearance!"

IF IT ISN'T PM IT ISN'T AN EVENING

National Distillers Products Corporation, New York, N. Y.
Blended Whiskey.   86 Proof.   70% Grain Neutral Spirits.

"TELEVISION PARTY," by Douglass Crockwell. Number 27 in the series "Home Life in America," by noted American illustrators.

Beer belongs...enjoy it

In this home-loving land of ours . . . in this America of kindliness, of friendship, of good-humored tolerance . . . perhaps no beverages are more "at home" on more occasions than good American beer and ale.

For beer and ale are the kinds of beverages Americans like. They belong—to pleasant living, to good fellowship, to sensible moderation. And our right to enjoy them, this too belongs—to our own American heritage of personal freedom.

AMERICA'S BEVERAGE OF MODERATION

"Between Innings" by Pruett Carter. *Number 112 in the Series "Home Life in America"*

When you're taking it easy—

What makes a glass of beer taste so good?

Malted barley—selected from America's finest crops—and containing certain important minerals that our bodies use up every day.

Tangy hops that are harvested only during the period of a few short weeks when their flavor is at its absolute height.

The way it "goes with everything" —the way it fits into the friendliness of American life—makes beer America's Beverage of Moderation.

Beer Belongs—Enjoy It!

"BASEBALL ON TELEVISION," by Glenn Grohe. Number 16 in the series "Home Life in America," by noted American illustrators.

*B*eer belongs...enjoy it

In this home-loving land of ours . . . in this America of kindliness, of friendship, of good-humored tolerance . . . perhaps no beverages are more "at home" on more occasions than good American beer and ale.

For beer is the kind of beverage Americans like. It belongs—to pleasant living, to good fellowship, to sensible moderation. And our right to enjoy it, this too belongs—to our own American heritage of personal freedom.

AMERICA'S BEVERAGE OF MODERATION

"OUT BY THE GOLDEN GATE," by Douglass Crockwell. Number 61 in the series "Home Life in America."

In this friendly, freedom-loving land
of ours — *beer belongs … enjoy it!*

*Beer and ale —
mealtime favorites*

AMERICA'S BEVERAGE OF MODERATION
Sponsored by the United States Brewers Foundation…Chartered 1862

"World Series U. S. A.," by John Falter.   Number 86 in the series "Home Life in America"

I*n this friendly, freedom-loving land of ours—Beer belongs . . . enjoy it!*

First down and pleasure to go!

EXCITING football and satisfying Corby's highballs—all in the comfort of your own 50-yard-line TV seat! How's that for pleasure on a crisp fall day? Flavorful, sociable Corby's, long an All-American favorite, is today more popular than ever. Try it. For fine whiskey taste, say "Corby's"—at home or in your favorite tavern.

Time to say CORBY'S

7

TELEVISION CELEBRITY –
On the Big Screen
but in *Front* of the Little Screen

TELEVISION CELEBRITY –
On the Big Screen
but in Front of the Little Screen

Television and celebrity are so nearly synonymous today it's hard to imagine that in the beginning the biggest celebrities couldn't be found on it. But that didn't stop print advertisers from connecting them with it.

From the 1940s through the 1950s, movie stars were contractually prevented from appearing on the small screen. Motion pictures suffered steady and eventually drastic drops in attendance after World War II, and studio heads blamed the concurrent rise of television as the cause. Believing that if people could see actors for free on television they would not also pay to see them in theaters, studio heads made sure their stars remained only on the big screen. But even if film stars couldn't appear on television sets, they could still *sell* them, a point the legal departments of motion picture studios regrettably overlooked. Magnavox jumped on this oversight with a vengeance, running an extensive series of celebrity ads from the early to mid-1950s that included Edgar (and little Candice) Bergen, Jerry Lewis with Dean Martin and Polly Bergen, Lizabeth Scott, Ray Milland, Helen Hayes, Ellen Drew, singer Ezio Pinza, performers Peter Lind Hayes and Mary Healy, and some of the cast and production personnel of then-current motion picture releases *Come Back, Little Sheeba* and *The Greatest Show on Earth,* featuring Burt Lancaster, Shirley Booth, Charlton Heston, Betty Hutton, and director extraordinaire, Cecil B. DeMille.

DEAN MARTIN and JERRY LEWIS • Marion Marshall, Polly Bergen • Starring in the Hal Wallis Motion Picture, "THAT'S MY BOY" • A Paramount Release

Join the Stars with *Magnavox* Big-Picture TV

YOU join mighty proud company when you move magnificent Magnavox Big-Picture Television into your living room. For Magnavox instruments are built to grace the finest homes. And Magnavox Big-Picture TV is the kind enjoyed by so many of the entertainment world's most hard-to-please experts. Owners tell us that the glorious, concert-hall tone of Magnavox and its noticeably clearer, sharper pictures are the envy of their neighborhoods. Magnavox combines advanced engineering—super-sensitive circuits, extra-powerful speakers and eye-restful filters—with stunning cabinetry of heirloom quality. Yet Magnavox values are without equal. Choose the perfect Magnavox for your proud home at one of the distinguished dealers listed in your classified telephone directory. Only stores famous for outstanding service are selected to sell Magnavox. The Magnavox Company, Fort Wayne 4, Indiana.

THE FRENCH PROVINCIAL (also shown above). AM-FM radio-phonograph in smart Savoy finish. Accommodates twenty-inch TV now or later.

the magnificent

Magnavox

television - radio - phonograph

BETTER SIGHT...BETTER SOUND...BETTER BUY

The Edgar Bergens watching the real-as-life performance
of Charlie McCarthy on Magnavox Belvedere 20-inch TV.

Magnavox the magnificent gift for all the family

One gift pleases everybody—a magnificent Magnavox! So why not make sure that everyone in your family will be tickled pink with what you give? Why not pool your Christmas spending money and buy one magnificent gift for all—the priceless gift of endless entertainment! Year in, year out your entire family will find your gift a source of daily pleasure and pride...as long as it's a Magnavox. And you, in turn, will find the right price for your budget—and the right cabinet design for your home—among the many superb models offered by Magnavox. Only America's finest stores are selected to sell Magnavox. See your classified telephone directory. The Magnavox Company, Fort Wayne 4, Indiana.

THE BELVEDERE (also shown above). AM-FM radio-phonograph in rich mahogany or blonde oak finish. Add superb Magnavox 20-inch TV now or later.

BETTER SIGHT...BETTER SOUND...BETTER BUY

the magnificent
Magnavox
television radio-phonograph

Color and Ultra High Frequency Units Readily Attachable

Hal Wallis, famous motion picture producer—
a Magnavox TV owner—says, "The warm color-tone
of the Chromatic Filter in my Magnavox provides
the finest TV picture I have ever seen."

Hal Wallis

Shirley Booth, Burt Lancaster and Hal Wallis look at film from Paramount motion picture,"Come Back Little Sheba"

Magnavox
chromatic television
brings you thrilling realism

The Magnavox Chromatic Filter, an innovation in television, provides a warm color-tone which brings you beautiful pictures and a striking illusion of dimension.

Contrasted with the cold harshness of conventional television, this achievement adds immeasurably to your TV enjoyment. In addition, the sense of realism given by Magnavox high-fidelity sound creates a feeling of intimacy with the performers that you never before have enjoyed in television.

While Magnavox is recognized as the finest TV, it actually costs less than other well-known brands. Direct-to-dealer selling saves you money. Your classified telephone book lists your nearest dealer. Go to his store at once for a thrilling demonstration of Magnavox Chromatic Television.

magnificent **Magnavox** *television*

EXCLUSIVE MAGNASCOPE BIG-PICTURE SYSTEM GIVES YOU:
1. Super Power to capture all the clarity and dimension of picture the TV camera is capable of transmitting! **2. Chromatic Optical Filter** to soften glaring electron beams and bring you pleasingly clear pictures without eye-strain. **3. Reflection Barrier** to deflect annoying glare and distracting reflections. **PLUS Magnavox High-Fidelity Sound** to supplement picture realism with a sound system of full dimensional qualities.

The Magnavox Company, Fort Wayne 4, Indiana

THE PROVINCIAL 24—Latest achievement in Big-Picture TV. New 24-inch screen with Chromatic Filter in a graceful fine-furniture cabinet of antiqued fruitwood. Two Magnavox speakers cover complete high-fidelity range. All-channel UHF-VHF continuous tuner built in.

167

MacRAE FAMILY AND FRIEND TAKE IT EASY IN McGREGOR SPORTSWEAR...TAKE IT EASY WITH GRAFLEX CAMER

All the MacRaes agree...years-ahead Westinghouse 22-inch* Color TV makes it the best Christmas ever!

Now in one set you get *both* —the biggest-of-all screen plus the most natural color ever to thrill your eyes! The big 22-inch* Westinghouse Picture Tube is powered by years-ahead PRECISIONEERED circuits that alone pick up so faithfully every shade and subtle tone of life itself. Black and White reception is brilliant...fully detailed, steady and sharp! And tuning is so easy...controls work just like ordinary Black and White sets.

Exclusive *rectangular* Picture Tube permits the slimmer, trimmer cabinets of Westinghouse Color TV, no larger than modern Black and White receivers. Above, Westinghouse 22-inch Color Set, Model 22T156...in Limed-Oak Grained Finish.

*Overall tube diagonal. Picture tube area 254 sq. in.

WATCH WESTINGHOUSE

8

TELEVISION IMPRINT –
Mother's Little Helper

TELEVISION IMPRINT –
Mother's Little Helper

Magazine cover and ad illustrations didn't always accurately reflect American life in the 1950s, but that didn't mean they didn't contain underlying truths. One type of television ad was particularly self-fulfilling: television as a substitute for wife and mother. Curiously, ad illustrations of families and their radios in the 1930s and 1940s never presented radio this way. This may well have been a sign of the times: husbands and fathers during that period were faced with their families' very real need to survive day to day in the face of joblessness, hunger, hard times, and war during the Depression and World War II. With the end of the war and a new flush economy, husbands and fathers could relax a little, and the new television set in the home was viewed as the perfect companion to kick back with on the sofa. Wives and mothers also had more free time on their hands, what with automatic washers, clothes driers, dishwashers, and ready-for-the-

oven frozen foods helping with domestic life. But with so much free time, families didn't turn their attentions to one another; they turned, spellbound, their eyes locked as if by a tractor beam, to the television set. And why not? The TV didn't nag about undone chores and was an agreeable partner who would play any game or entertainment you wanted without objection. You only had to turn the channel. Television was comforting and always ready with a joke, cartoon, movie, or sporting event. You only had to turn it on. No wife or mother could compete with such immediate gratification.

Television was often characterized in ads as the "other woman," a siren beckoning males of all ages. But this was a far cry from providing actual sexual comfort—until times had changed to such a degree that sexually explicit programming could be found on it. Television would come to be known as the "boob tube"—but it was the perspective of the infant, not the husband, that was meant.

The Saturday Evening

POST

April 21, 1956 — 15¢

HOW TO MANAGE TEEN-AGERS
By Governor Collins of Florida

**Ernie Banks of
the Chicago Cubs**

The Saturday Evening

POST

April 29, 1961 — 15¢

How to Bet the Horses
By TED ATKINSON

DEAN MARTIN By PETE MARTIN

KANSAS By JOHN BIRD

SECRETARY of LABOR GOLDBERG on the UNEMPLOYMENT CRISIS

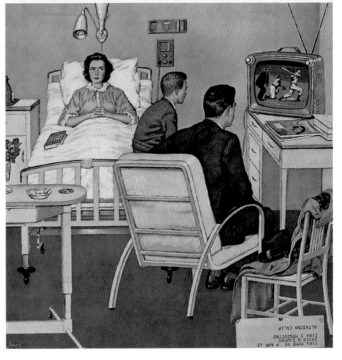

The Saturday Evening

POST

November 9, 1957 — 15¢

**HOW TO WIN
AT POKER**

By Herbert O. Yardley

Michigan's Soapy Williams

The Saturday Evening

POST

October 8, 1960 — 15¢

**THE CASE FOR THE
REPUBLICANS**
By Sen. Hugh Scott

NEXT WEEK: THE CASE FOR THE DEMOCRATS

BARUCH: THE ROOSEVELT YEARS

ACKNOWLEDGMENTS

The magazine covers, marketing materials, and advertisements in this book are from my personal collection. But the genesis for the project originated with my editor, Alan Rapp. Alan worked with designer John Barretto, who is responsible for the beautiful finished layout; copy editor Jeff Campbell, who made great text suggestions; and Leslie Davisson, whose manuscript administration was splendid from beginning to end. Thank you Alan, John, Jeff, and Leslie for all of your time and hard work involved with this project.

Others closer to home also deserve a note of thanks: Paul L'Esperance for supporting my writing endeavors and entertaining and taking care of the world's oldest (29 years—and still counting!) crotchety cockatiel, Vulture; fellow writer and longtime friend Kyle Counts for reviewing the initial manuscript; and my attorney, Paul S. Levine, for "the deal." Lastly, my parents, John and Susan Kosareff, gifted me with a large professional scanner, which allowed me to digitally retrieve and restore the television images in these pages from their oversized sources before another avenue of our cultural history was lost.

Thank you to all.